India: An Introduction is a highly [...]
complex, ancient civilization, by [...]
and journalists.

Khushwant Singh tells the story [...]
earliest time to the present day. Through broad, vivid strokes he recounts
the saga of the upheavals of a subcontinent over five millennia, and how
their interplay over the centuries has moulded the India of today.
Moreover, Khushwant Singh offers perceptive insights into everything
Indian that may catch one's eye or arouse one's curiosity: its ethnic
diversity, religions, customs, philosophy, art and culture, political
currents and the galaxy of men and women who have helped shape its
intricately inlaid mosaic. He is also an enlightening guide to much else:
India's extensive and varied architectural splendours, its art and classical
literature.

Khushwant Singh's own fascination with the subject is contagious,
showing through on every page, and in every sidelight that he presents.
India: An Introduction holds strong appeal for just about anyone who has
more than a passing interest in the country: Indians as well as those who
are drawn to it from farther afield. And for a traveller, this work is that rare
companion: erudite, intelligent and lively.

Khushwant Singh is easily the most widely read author in India today. His
weekly columns are reproduced by over fifty journals in all the regional
languages of the country. He has done different things at different times:
practised law, diplomacy and politics; taught comparative religion at
Princeton and Swarthmore; and edited *The Illustrated Weekly of India*
and *The Hindustan Times*. He has written regularly for several European
and American journals including *The New York Times*. He has also edited
and translated a number of literary works.

Author of eighty-nine books, Khushwant Singh is best known for his work
of fiction, *Train to Pakistan,* and his two-volume *History of the Sikhs,*
which is still considered the most authoritative writing on the subject. His
acerbic pen, his wit and humour, and, most of all, his ability to laugh at
himself, have ensured him immense popularity over the years.

He was a Member of Parliament from 1980 to 1986. Among other
honours, he was awarded the Padma Bhushan in 1974 by the president of
India (he returned the decoration in 1984 in protest against the Union
government's siege of the Golden Temple, Amritsar).
He lives in New Delhi.

INDIA
AN INTRODUCTION

Khushwant Singh

HarperCollins *Publishers* India
a joint venture with

New Delhi

HarperCollins *Publishers* **India**
a joint venture with
The India Today Group

Copyright © Khushwant Singh 1974, 1990

Published in hardback 2003
Published in paperback 2006

ISBN 13: 97-88-172-23-6595
ISBN 10: 81-7223-659-X

HarperCollins *Publishers*
1A Hamilton House Connaught Place, New Delhi 110001, India
77-85 Fulham Palace Road, London W6 8JB, United Kingdom
Hazelton Lanes, 55 Avenue Road, Suite 2900, Toronto, Ontario M5R 3L2
and 1995 Markham Road, Scarborough, Ontario M1B 5M8, Canada
25 Ryde Road, Pymble, Sydney, NSW 2073, Australia
31 View Road, Glenfield, Auckland 10, New Zealand
10 East 53rd Street, New York NY 10022, USA
Typeset in 11/14 Classical Garamond

Typeset in 10.5/13 Utopia
by Nikita Overseas Pvt. Ltd.

Printed and bound at Thomson Press (India) Ltd.

Contents

Introduction

I learnt more about India teaching Indian history and religions to American students at Princeton, Swarthmore and Hawaii than I could have attending lectures in an Indian University. I was a poor student and imbibed very little learning from my professors. When the rules were reversed and instead of sitting in class among students I had to face them alone standing on the podium, I had to garner all the information I could, poring over books in the library, arranging it in a presentable order and prepare myself to answer questions that might be put to me. It proved to be a most daunting and exhausting task. The seminar system which had just come into vogue during my teaching years at American Universities required even more study and face to face confrontation with young and bright minds full of enquiry and passion for learning. I can echo the opinion of Rabbi Hillel when he said,

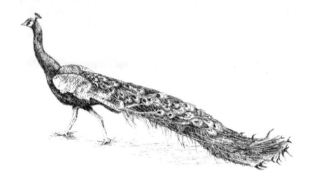

"I have learned much from my teachers, still more from my colleagues, but from my pupils more than from all of them."

Fortunately I kept notes of lectures I had to prepare. Some years after I had quit teaching and taken up the editorship of *The Illustrated Weekly of India* in Bombay, I found these notes helpful in writing articles for my own journal and several others when I was commissioned to write for *The New York Times.* Since these articles were not for learned audiences but for readers of newspapers and journals I had to teach myself how to communicate with the common man in the street: to explain Hinduism to people who can't be bothered to read the Vedas, Upanishads, the epics and the Gita; to explain Islam to non-Muslims who are never likely to read a biography of Prophet Mohammed, the Quran and the Hadith. And so on. At the same time I felt there were simple things like ethnic names, customs and rituals, peculiar dresses which marked religious communities from each other. Why, for instance, Iyers who are Saivites wear a particular form of caste-mark on their foreheads than Iyengars who are Vaishnavites; why all Sikhs are Singhs but not all Singhs are Sikh; why Sikhs wear turbans and what, if anything, the colour of their headwear signifies; why some Jains go stark naked while other do not; why all are strict vegetarians and some even refrain from eating vegetables like potatoes, onions and garlic, which grow under the ground.

It was after going over my college lectures many times, adding to them and bringing them uptodate that I decided to put them in the form of a book, a sort of introduction to India – its colourful peoples, its potted history, its religions, its politics and its literature. Specialists may find fault with such a broad sweep. But this book is not meant for them but for the intelligent, enquiring layman who wants to know more about India and has no time to pore over large tomes of books of learning.

It may appear like an instant-India version of instant coffee, but I hope there is more to it than that. If it lights a spark of interest in my reader's mind so that he would like to further pursue his studies in India, my hopes will have been fulfilled.

New Delhi   Khushwant Singh

1

The Land and The People

*T*ake a Look at a map of the world and gauge the size of India. It is the seventh largest country in the world and, after China, the second largest in Asia. Covering an area of 1,127,000 square miles, it extends over 2,000 miles from north to south and 1,700 miles from east to west. It has land frontiers with Pakistan, Russia, China, Bangladesh, Nepal and Burma which stretch over 8,200 miles across deserts, mountains and tropical forests. Its coastline is over 3,500 miles long.

India has three major zones – the Himalayas, the Indo-Gangetic plain and the Deccan plateau. Before the creation of Pakistan, the subcontinent had a geographical unity, with mountain ranges forming the frontiers of the north and the west. The importance of these mountains lay in their impassability. They are

The Himalayas

the highest in the world – Mount Everest rising to 29,028 feet – and most of them are snowbound throughout the year, as indeed, their name, *Hima* (snow) *alaya* (the abode) signifies. Of greater historical importance than the towering heights and the perennial snows were the few passes which made the Himalayas passable and, like sluice gates of a dam, provided regular inlets for the hordes that lived on the other side. Passes like the Bolan, Khurram and Khyber are in the north-west; there are many others which link India with Tibet. These passes were known to nomads and shepherds who grazed their flocks of sheep and goats in the valleys, to tradesmen who brought their caravans of merchandise through them and, of course, to marauders who used them to invade and loot the rich plains of India.

The history of India is monotonous and tragic repetition of invasions through the Himalayan passes. The timing was fixed with calendar-like precision. The invader got his forces together just before autumn, crossed the passes before snowfall and swept down on the Indian plains in early winter when the skies were blue, the air cool and fragrant with the smell of mustard, green wheat and sugarcane. Most of the battles between the invaders and the Indians were fought in the Punjab and if the invaders were victorious, which they often were, they spent the winter months systematically looting the cities – Lahore, Karnal, Panipat, Delhi, Mathura, Agra. Before the summer's heat came on, they carried away the harvested winter crops, retraced their steps, and disappeared into the mountain passes through which they had come.

While the Himalayas gave Indians the illusion of being guarded by an impassable wall, the Indo-Gangetic plain gave them the illusion of owning an inexhaustible granary. About 70,000 square miles in area, the plain is one of the world's longest alluvium tracts. Cities, towns and villages cover it, one within sight of the other. The States of Uttar Pradesh, Bihar and West Bengal, for instance, have about six times the density of population obtaining in the United States of America. When the monsoon fails, districts of eastern Uttar Pradesh, Bihar and Orissa become like the dust bowl of Rajasthan, unable to feed their millions.

The third great divide is the Deccan plateau. The region is like a vast triangle; the low-lying ghats running along the sea coast form two sides, while the hill ranges of the Vindhya and Satpuras, with the rivers Narmada and Tapti, mark it off from the north. Though the region has geographical identity, it is inhabited by two racial groups. The northern half, describing itself as Deccani, speaks languages which are closely related. The southern half is inhabited by Dravidians speaking Dravidian languages: Telugu, Tamil, Kannada and Malayalam. Indians talk of these three parts of India as the head, the torso and the groin-and-legs of the one entity that is India. They visualise it as Mother India with her head in the snowy Himalayas, her arms stretched from the Punjab to Assam, her ample bosom and middle (the Indian concept of feminine beauty requires a woman to be big-breasted and heavy-hipped) resting on the Indo-Gangetic plain and the Deccan, and her feet bathed by the waters of the Indian Ocean. Sri Lanka is like a lotus-petalled foot-stool. This deified configuration of Mother India is often depicted by Indian artists as goddess Lakshmi, the goddess of plenty, or Saraswati, the patron goddess of the arts. In 1947, the Indian subcontinent had its eastern and western extremes lopped off to make the two wings of the State of Pakistan. Thereafter Mother India assumed the shape of a Venus de Milo.

Climate and the Seasons

India has a wide range of climates. In the deserts of Rajasthan the summer temperature can rise to 125°F in the shade, while most of the Himalayas are perpetually snowbound with sub-freezing temperatures. The Deccan, however, is temperate.

The monsoon is the chief factor in India's climate. It consists of a short winter season of rains in December or January (on which depends the winter crop) and a prolonged heavy downpour lasting from June to the end of September. The summer monsoon floods the rivers and inundates the plains, often submerging thousands of villages. But it also irrigates India's rice and jute fields. The intensity of the summer monsoon

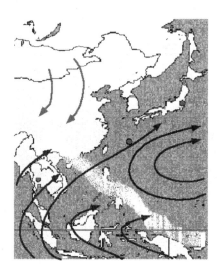

Monsoon

varies from region to region. The town of Cherapunji in Meghalaya has the highest annual rainfall in the world, 500 inches; while some districts in Saurashtra seldom get more than 3 inches of rain and are, as a consequence, virtually lifeless.

Broadly, India has five seasons: summer, monsoon (derived from the Arabic *mausem*, meaning "season of the rains"), autumn, winter and spring. The summer and monsoon account for over half the year. During these months, when searing heat is followed by torrential rains, Indians can do little besides find shade or shelter. This partly explains the Indian's indolence and lethargy. Epidemics of malaria, typhus, typhoid, cholera and innumerable other diseases, which further enervate the people, come in the wake of the monsoon. And if the rains are scanty, crops wither and there is famine. This is yet another factor adding to the Indian's predisposition to ascribe everything to the whims of the gods, to predestination and therefore, being resigned to his fate. The writer, Nirad C. Chaudhuri, for instance, claims that most of the Indians' mental and physical sluggishness is due to the climate and their stodgy diet. As the title of Mr Chaudhuri's book suggests, India is the *Continent of Circe*, because those who make their homes here are sooner or later turned into swine.

Minerals

India has amongst the world's largest deposits of coal, which though not of very good quality, is nevertheless found in great abundance. She also has large deposits of iron. Petroleum and gas are being discovered and Indians are currently pumping out more than 20 million tonnes of oil every year. India produces 75 per cent of the world's mica and, after Russia, the world's largest quantity of manganese. Though not so rich in gold, silver, lead, chromite or copper, India does have good quantities of uranium and also varieties of rare earths.

Flora and Fauna

Though the climate may be enervating, at least it gives India a vast variety of flora and fauna. India is, after China, the world's largest producer of rice. It now produces enough wheat, millet, maize and barley to feed its vast population, even leaving a surplus for export. Cash crops like tea, coffee, jute, sugarcane and oilseeds are also raised in which again, next to China, India is the most fecund.

Fifteen per cent of India's land is still covered by forests of teak, sal, fir, pine and a host of other varieties of trees, giving the country a considerable wealth in timber. The forests are being rapidly depleted, but an organised drive to plant more trees during the *Vanamahotsava* (tree-planting) months of the monsoon may prevent them from being turned into deserts.

At one time India had as rich and varied fauna as that of tropical Africa: elephants, rhinoceros, bison, herds of deer, lions, tigers, panthers, bears, hyenas, wolves – just about everything you could name in the animal, bird or serpent kingdom. It still has the remnants of most of these varieties. But men have taken a terrible and senseless toll of wildlife and many rare species like the cheetah, leopard, chinkara deer, the maneless lion and the Imperial bustard are almost extinct.

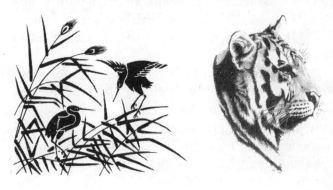

Flora and Fauna

With an estimated 150 million cows, 40 million buffaloes, 50 million goats and sheep, India has the largest number of milch cattle in the world. The Indian cow, however, yields very little milk. Most Indians drink buffalo or goat milk. The chief by-product of cattle is dung which, instead of being used as manure, is mixed with straw or coal-dust and burnt as fuel. This is beginning to change, as India has begun to produce fertilisers, hydroelectric power and refined oil.

The People

In July 1981 the population of India was estimated at 685.2 million, going up at the rate of nearly 25 per cent in 10 years. Attempts at family planning have only been moderately successful. India is often described as an ethnic museum. Although the dividing lines between the different races are never clear, at least six different racial types can be discerned in different regions.

The oldest Indian racial group are the *adi* (first) *vasis* (settlers), the aboriginals of India. They are somewhat negroid in their features and till recently lived in jungles and mountains in a boomerang-shaped area extending from Assam in the north-east right down to Kanyakumari. They belong to many different tribes and their mode of living varies from region to region.

The next large ethnic group is described as Dravidians. They inhabit the southern half of the Deccan Plateau. It is assumed that it was the Dravidians who first drove out the aboriginals from the fertile plains into the forests and mountains, as later they in their turn were driven southwards by the Aryans who came to India from somewhere in Central Europe.

The Aryans inhabit the Indo-Gangetic valley. They were originally of Caucasian stock: blond, blue-eyed and spoke the same language as their European kinsmen. Latin and Sanskrit still have many common words and a similar grammatical structure. Eire, for Ireland, and

Iran, for Persia, are believed to be derived from the word "Arya". Since the Aryan domination of India from about 2000 BC onwards, India came to be known as *Aryavarta*, the land of the Aryans, or *Bharatavarsha* the land of the Bharatas, an Aryan tribe which settled in the land between the Indus and the Ganges.

The Arab Semites followed the Aryans. Then came the Mongols and the Europeans. The Semites and the Europeans mingled with the local population and did not occupy any defined geographical region. So did the Mongols, but in certain outlying regions of north-eastern India, Mongoloid strains are still discernible.

Languages

The mixture of races produced a large number of languages. Linguists have listed 845 dialects and 225 distinct languages. The Constitution of India recognises 15 major languages including Sanskrit. If there was a Tower of Babel, India is that polygot tower today. The most widely spoken language is Hindi, or Hindustani. Over 30 per cent of the population speak or understand some form of this language. Hindi, or Hindustani, has therefore been recognised and developed as the national language.

Most Indian languages fall into two broad categories: those of Sanskrit origin spoken in the northern half of India and those of Dravidian paternity spoken in the south. The northern half has many common words; southern languages, though liberally infused with Sanskrit terminology, are distinct from the northern languages.

India has also produced its own type of "Indian English". English has taken several thousand words from Indian languages: bungalow, verandah, chutney, admiral, the word "Blighty" for England itself. Indians have taken many more words from English and twisted them into Indian shapes. It is known as the Hobson-Jobson and has a sizeable dictionary of its own. The way Indians pronounce English words baffles other English-speaking peoples. It is odd, but while it is difficult to tell what part of the country an Indian comes from if he is speaking one of the Indian languages, a few words spoken in English will immediately reveal his state and sometimes his status as well.

Religions

Eight different religions are followed in India; Hinduism, Islam, Christianity, Sikhism, Buddhism, Jainism, Zoroastrianism and Judaism.

About 83 per cent of the population being Hindus, India could be described as a Hindu country except that Hinduism evades definition and its varieties are many.

The Muslims come next, forming over 11 per cent of the population. Thus after Indonesia and Bangladesh, India has the world's third largest population of Muslims. There are a few regions, such as the valley of Kashmir and some districts of Kerala and Uttar

Pradesh, where they outnumber other religious denominations.

After the Muslims came the Christians who form 2.3 per cent. Christianity came to India earlier than it came to Europe. But it spread only during the Portuguese, Dutch, French and British occupation. The Christians are mainly concentrated in Kerala, Goa and the tribal belt, notably in Assam, Bihar, Orissa and Madhya Pradesh. Like their co-religionists elsewhere, they are divided into many denominations: Roman Catholic, Syrian and Protestant (mainly Presbyterian and Baptist).

The Sikhs number around 16 million and constitute 2 per cent of the population. They are, however, concentrated in one area, East Punjab, where they are in a majority. Unlike other religious groups who speak the languages of the regions they inhabit, the Sikhs speak one language, Punjabi.

Buddhism, though born in India, left its homeland for many centuries. Its return to India is a recent phenomenon. India has around 4.5 million neo-Buddhists, chiefly converts from what are known as the lower, untouchable castes of Hindus. Indian Buddhists are, therefore, more a sociological than a religious phenomenon.

The remaining religious groups are of very little numerical importance. The Jains, now virtually indistinguishable from the Hindus, number 3 million. Zoroastrians, or Parsis as they are known in India,

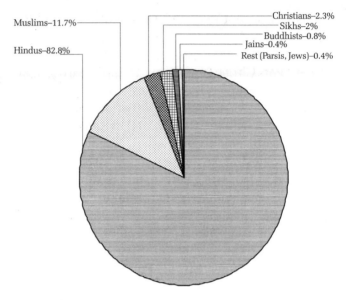

Muslims–11.7%

Hindus–82.8%

Christians–2.3%
Sikhs–2%
Buddhists–0.8%
Jains–0.4%
Rest (Parsis, Jews)–0.4%

Main Religions of India

number less than 100,000 and are concentrated in the cities, chiefly Bombay. Their importance is due to the fact that they are the most go-ahead people in the country and control some of the biggest industrial enterprises. The Jews now number less than 5,000. The oldest Indian synagogue is in Cochin's "Jew Town" and there are Bene Israeli Jews in Maharashtra. Although anti-Semitism has never been known of in India, large numbers of Indian Jews have emigrated to Israel.

India has always been, and is to this day, primarily an agricultural country. About seventy-two per cent of its population lives in the villages. In recent years there has been a noticeable shift of the population towards industrial towns and cities. It has only 187 cities with a population of over one hundred thousand – Bombay, Calcutta, Delhi, Madras, Hyderabad, Ahmedabad, Bangalore, Kanpur and others.

2

Hinduism-1

*T*he vast majority of the population of India are Hindus. If Jains, Buddhists and Sikhs are reckoned as Hindus, and there are good enough reasons for so doing, then almost 87 per cent of India is Hindu. So it is on Hinduism that we should concentrate.

Religion plays a very important part in Indian life. But the claim that Indians are more spiritually minded or other-worldly than any other people in the world is arrant nonsense. There is more talk about money and material things in India than in the so-called materialist societies. Nevertheless, religion and ritual pervade the lives of Indians more than they do the lives of most other people. Religious considerations are for instance, sometimes more vital than economic factors. Take the recurrent spectacle of famine. A

Hindu believing in *ahimsa* – non-violence – and the sanctity of life, even if he was on the verge of death, would rather die than slaughter an animal to feed himself.

The phenomenon of the cow is another good example. Most thinking Hindus will concede that the country has too many cows, they yield very little milk, thousands of them roam the streets and the fields, famished and uncared for; it would be better to reduce their numbers and use their flesh as food. But when it comes to practical proposals to do so, they shrink back with horror.

The Constitution of India has been drafted by highly erudite Hindus, many of whom had been educated at American and British Universities and eaten their fill of beef-steaks and veal escallops when they were abroad. But when it came to putting it down on paper, they felt compelled to insert a direction clause in the Constitution providing for the protection of cows. This clause is ingeniously worded so that outsiders might not snigger and call them backward:

> The State shall endeavour to organise agriculture and animal husbandry on modern and scientific lines and shall, in particular, take steps for preserving and improving the breeds, and prohibiting the slaughter of cows and calves and other milch and draught cattle.

Indian religions (and by that we mean the Hindu family of religions) approach human problems from quite a different angle than the Judaic religions: Judaism, Christianity and Islam. The simplest way of understanding this different approach is to examine the three kinds of relationships that all religions provide for, viz., Man's relationship to God, his Maker, Sustainer and Destroyer; Man's relationship to his fellow men, i.e., his rights and obligations to the society in which he lives; and Man's relationship to himself, i.e., his conscience.

All religions have something to say about these relationships; it is in the choice of what they emphasise that we can discern their different approaches to common problems. The Judaic family of religions lay greater emphasis on Man's relationship to his fellow men; the Hindu family of religions, on the other hand, stress Man's relationship to himself. Thus Judaism, Christianity and Islam have many dos and don'ts, the kind summarised in the Commandments: Thou shalt not kill; Thou shalt not covet another's goods; Thou shalt not commit adultery, etc. The Hindu family of religions emphasise the realisation of knowledge (*atmavidya*), conquest of the self and the importance of achieving peace of mind.

The Western man of religion is the missionary, the do-gooder, the boy scout. The Hindu's paradigm of religion is the Sadhu or the yogi who meditates in solitude with total unconcern with what is happening to his neighbours. Important practical consequences flow from these different attitudes. The Hindu is inward-looking, narcissistic and stuck in the *cul-de-sac* of the self. The Westerner is outward-looking, concerned with improving the community in which he lives.

We have said before that Hinduism defies definition. The word Hindu does not appear in any of the sacred texts of the Hindus. Hinduism has no prophet or messiah in the sense Jews, Christians and Muslims have prophets or messiahs. It has no one sacred book like the Torah, and Bible or the Quran. It has no specific creed. It is, as Dr Radhakrishnan, the eminent interpreter of Hinduism, says, "a name without any content". He goes on to ask, "Is it a museum of beliefs; a medley of rites, or a mere map, a geographical location?" And continues, "Its content, if any, has altered from age to age, from community to community. It meant one thing in the Vedic period, another in the Brahmanical, a third in the Buddhist – one to Saivite, another to Vaishnavite and Sakta."

Macnicol, another eminent Indologist, described it as an "encyclopaedia of religions … an amalgam of often contradictory beliefs and practices held together in one by certain powerful ideas and a system of social regulations." It is, as pointed out by yet another Hindu scholar, Sen, "more like a tree than a building designed by one architect".

Hinduism can be examined from three aspects: the philosophic, the sociological, i.e., the division of society into different castes, and the popular or folk

Hinduism – the religion as practised by the vast majority of Hindus. But it should be borne in mind that chronologically it should be in the reverse order because folk Hinduism, the pantheon of gods and goddesses, worship of trees, snakes and the elements of nature, came first; the caste system which was a product of the intermingling of the animist aboriginal with the Aryan came second, and the works of religious philosophy came last.

Hindu Religious Philosophy

Hindu religious literature was produced in successive periods of history and can be divided into different categories.

The earliest was the Vedic period, assumed to be between 2500 BC and 600 BC. There are four Vedas or books of knowledge: Rig, Yajur, Sama and Atharva. They were composed by scholars whose identity remains unknown except for the fact that they must have been of the Aryan race.

The oldest and most important of the Vedas is the Rig Veda. The others are mere litanies, rules of ritual, techniques of meditation and magical incantations.

The Rig Veda

The Rig is a sizeable compilation of hymns. Internal

evidence proves that at least a hundred years must have elapsed between the composition of the first and the last verse. Even when it was completed, the Aryans had got no further into India than the river Jumna; there is only one reference in the Rig Veda to the river Ganges.

The second period is known as the epic (or Puranic) period. It was during this period, between 600 BC and AD 200 that the great epics of Hinduism, the Mahabharata and the Ramayana were composed. It was also during this time that the two dissenting schools, Jainism and Buddhism, arose in north-eastern India, showing thereby that by this time the Aryan tribes had spread over the Indo-Gangetic plain.

The period also saw the flowering of Hindu philosophical thought to its fullness. Commentaries on the Vedas, known as the Upanishads, were written. There are almost 200 Upanishads. The Bhagvad Gita, considered the greatest piece of Hindu religious writing, is a chapter in the story of the Mahabharata.

During the third period, ending in AD 1000, many schools of Hindu religious philosophy flourished. By now, Islam had established itself in northern India. Hindu schools and philosophers migrated to the South where they continued to write treatises and commentaries right upto the seventeenth century.

We shall first deal with the development of Hindu religious thought in the Rig Veda and the Upanishads, then give a brief account of the Mahabharata, including the Gita and the Ramayana. We shall follow up with a discussion on the Puranas; the origins, incidence and extent of the caste system and finally, sum up with Hinduism as it is practised by the common people today.

The *Rig Veda* (Praise of Wisdom)

The Rig Veda, as already stated, is an Aryan composition. There were, however, people before the Aryans with religious beliefs and practices of their own. First there were the aboriginals; then the Dravidians who overcame the aboriginals and were, in their turn, overcome by the Aryans. Since it took the Rig Veda many decades to be completed, we can assume that while its earlier chapters are purely Aryan, the later chapters were influenced by Dravidian and aboriginal beliefs.

We do not know very much of the religious beliefs of the aboriginals as they had not learnt the art of writing. The only source material that has come down to us is their folk songs and magical rites to propitiate objects which they, as children of the forest, feared. Thus we know that they worshipped *Nagas* (snakes), *Simha* (the lion or the tiger); spirits of the dead, trees like the peepul and the banyan (both species of the ficus) in which spirits were believed to reside; epidemics like smallpox personified into the goddess Seetala. Phenomena that the aboriginal dreaded, they propitiated by offering sacrifices of animals such as oxen or fowls. The propitiatory rites were performed by a magic man. If the aboriginals believed in God, they probably visualised him as one of their own kind, a black God. All the religious practices of the aboriginals including their belief in the black God (reincarnated by the Aryans as Krishna), have come down to us and are as much in evidence today as they were in 3000 BC.

Our knowledge of the Dravidians' beliefs and practices is more extensive. In their cities, excavated in the 1920s, were found seals and figurines which tell us something of their religion. We have the figure of the Earth goddess – Devi – in an advanced stage of pregnancy; the symbolic representation of her genitals in *yoni* rings. We have the male counterpart of Devi in the form of a horned bull who, as the god of the kingdom, was Pasupati, the lord of beasts.

At some time in Dravidian history the bull and its phallus came apart. Siva emerged as the lord of Devi; the bull *nandi* became his mount; *linga,* his phallus, the symbol of potency. Siva and Devi began to appear in conjunction, with the *linga* rising in the middle of the *yoni,* to represent the creative aspect of God. The trees of the aboriginals, the peepul and the banyan, became the abodes of the deities. In addition to all these, Dravidian figurines have ascetics with matted locks, the conch-shell as an article for use in religious ritual and women wearing *sindoor* (vermilion) in the parting of their hair. All the Dravidian symbolism persists in the Hinduism of today.

On this aboriginal-Dravidian scene arrived the Aryans. We have reason to believe that they were worshippers of natural phenomena: *agni* (fire), *prithvi* (earth), *dyau* (sky), *indra* (thunder), *surya* (sun), *ushas* (aurora, daughter of the dawn and lady of light) and *vayu* (wind). They also considered *vak* (speech) as a gift from the gods. They had little inhibition against assimilating animism and worship of trees practised by the aboriginals and the Dravidians to their own deification of nature. Hymns to the elements elevated to the status of gods appear in the early portions of the Rig Veda.

The next step was to elevate some gods above the others by a process known as henotheism. Thus Varuna was elevated to the status of the director of natural or moral order prevailing in the universe; Visvakarma became the creator; Purusha, the primal person; Vishnu, the preserver of all that exists, became pre-eminent, the God among gods.

At the same time the Aryans began to speculate on how the universe came into existence and toy with the idea of one supreme God who was creator, preserver and destroyer. The hymn of creation in the Rig Veda deals with the genesis of the universe. But mark the recurring note of doubt:

> Non-being then existed not nor being.
> There was no air, nor sky that is beyond it.
> What was concealed? Wherein? In whose protection?

And was there deep, unfathomable water?

> Death then existed not, nor life immortal.
> Of neither night nor day was there any token.
> By its inherent force the one breathed windless.
> No other thing than that beyond existed.

Darkness there was at first by darkness hidden,
Without distinctive marks, this all was water
That which, becoming, by void was covered.
That one by force of heat came into being.

> Desire entered the one in the beginning.
> It was the earliest seed, of thought the product.
> The sages searching in their hearts with wisdom
> Found out the bond of being and non-being.

Their ray extended light across the darkness
But was the one above or was it under?
Creative force there was, and fertile power.
Below was energy, above was impulse.

> Who knows for certain? Who shall declare it?
> Whence was it born, and whence came this creation?
> Gods were born after this world's creation;
> Then who can know from whence it has risen?

No one knoweth whence creation has arisen
And whether He has or has not produced it,
He who surveys it in the highest heaven.
He only knows or haply He may know not.

(*Tradition of Indian Philosophy*, Radhakrishnan & Moore, pp 23-24.)

The element of doubt echoes more clearly in the hymns to Prajapati (Lord of the peoples) wherein the author questions the supremacy of any one God. "What God with our oblations shall we worship?" he asks at the end of each hymn.

The Rig Veda also posits two more questions: Is there a law governing the cosmos? Is there a law governing human society? Yes, answers the author of one of the hymns. There is indeed – *rta* (repetition) which maintains order in our universe. From this cosmic law we can derive *dharma*, the code of conduct for human society, and ethical concepts like *daya* (kindness), *dan* (charity), etc.

Authors of the Rig Veda also speculated about our disposition after death. We either go to *Vaikuntha* (heaven), or the abode of Yama, the god of death and "the gatherer of people".

Theories about God, universe and life after death were not accepted by all the authors of the Rig Veda. Some aired their scepticism in no uncertain terms. "There is no Indra. Who hath beheld him?" demanded the composer of the hymn to Indra. He was derisive of the Brahmin priests' claim to knowledge of the truth: "Frogs have filled up their voices," he said.

The most remarkable thing about the Rig Veda is the fact that it records the views of a people who more than 3000 years ago engaged in speculation about the nature of the creator, the ways and wherefores of birth, life and death, with open minds free of any trace of bigotry and with sophistication not known to other religious systems till much later.

The process of speculation is carried further by the Upanishads.

The Upanishads

The Upanishads, as the etymology of the word shows (*upa* = near, *ni* = down, *shad* sit, i.e., sit down near me), consist of dialogues between teacher and pupil. They are, as has been stated, almost 200 in number. But only about a dozen need to be noticed by us. They were written between the eighth and seventh centuries BC by savants whose identity, save where the book is named after them, is not known.

Reality is both objective (*brahman*) and subjective (*atman*). It is another way of saying, as in Christianity, that "I and my Father are One" and "the kingdom of God is within you". Our inability to see that the self and God are a unity and not two separate things is because we are deluded by *maya* (illusion) into a sense of duality (*dwaita*). Reality is more than omnipresent: all that is, is a manifestation of Reality.

In the Chhandogya, which is one of the best known of the Upanishads, the teacher asks his pupil to get the fruit of a banyan tree, cut it to extract its seed and then split the tiny seed itself. The eye sees nothing within the seed. "From the essence in the seed which you cannot see," says the teacher, "comes in truth this vast banyan tree ... an invisible and subtle essence is the spirit of the whole universe. That is Reality. That is *atman. Tat Tvam Asi* – Thou Art That."

Reality cannot be described except in negatives: *neti, neti*, not this, not this. Reality is beyond description because it is at once above all qualities (*nirguna*) and when it assumes the role of a personal God (*Ishvara*) has all qualities in it (*saguna*). Despite the admitted ineffability of Reality, authors of some of the Upanishads tried to put it into words. The *Isa*, the shortest of the Upanishads, with only eighteen hymns, describes all-pervading Reality in the following words:

> It moves, it moves not
> It is far and it is near
> It is within all this.
> And it is outside all this.

(*Tradition of Indian Philosophy*, Radhakrishnan & Moore, p 40, verse 5.)

The *Mundaka* (shaven like a sanyasi or hermit, hence shorn of ignorance) states: "Not by sight, speech, senses, austerity or work ... not by instruction, intellect or learning can we comprehend Reality, for human knowledge is limited whereas Reality is without limit." (Radhakrishnan & Moore, p 64, verse 8.) "Into blind darkness enter they that worship ignorance, into darkness greater than that those that delight in knowledge," states the Isa Upanishad.

Reality cannot be comprehended by the senses because it is the source of all the senses – of speech it is the word, of the eye the light, of the ear the sound, of taste the tongue, of body the touch.

Reality that is God, though indefinable, has three components: it is *sat* (truth), *chid* (understanding), and *anand* (bliss).

Although Reality or God is beyond the reach of thought or reason, it can be experienced "in the ecstasy of an awakening which opens the door to life eternal". (Kena Upanishad.) To experience God is to become God.

The goal of human endeavour should be to experience and thus become God. To achieve this men and women should discipline their lives and bend all they have, their senses, learning, thinking and actions – above all, their capacity to love, in the pursuit of God. According to the Kena Upanishad, the aim of life should be *tadvanam*, "end of love-longing".

How do we go about this business of the realisation of Reality that is God? First of all we must acquire a teacher, a guru. The guru is the disciple's (*chela's*) mentor, father and closest friend. All the Upanishads emphasise the guru-*chela* relationship by adopting the Platonic dialogue form of instruction: the questions are posed by the disciple and answered by the guru. The guru will point out which of the three paths is best for his disciple to reach his goal: whether he should pursue the path of *gyan* (knowledge of) *karma* (good deeds) devotion (bhakti). Discipline is of paramount importance. The *katha*, one of the more philosophical of the Upanishads, is in the form of a dialogue between Yama, the god of death, and the seeker-student, Nachiketa. Yama is asked to explain what happens to a man when he dies. Yama answers the question in a lengthy exposition emphasising the need for discipline to obtain knowledge, using charioteering as his simile. Yama equates the body to the chariot, the mind to the reins, reason to the charioteer, the senses to the horses and the human soul, that is you, to the passenger. The journey consists of several stages. We start by learning to control our senses, then to the realisation that objects perceived by the senses are illusory. Having reckoned with the senses we proceed to control our minds by cleansing them of worldly dross and make them capable of pure reasoning. The remaining stages come as a matter of course: we comprehend the nature of the spirit within us and its equation with the Supreme Spirit.

Samadhi

The necessity of samadhi (meditation) in absolute peace and quiet, with no other thought except that of attaining union (Yoga) with God, becomes the chief exercise of life. "There is something beyond our mind which abides in silence within our mind. It is the supreme mystery beyond thought," says the Maitreyi Upanishad.

The Upanishads say much more than the points summarised above. They speak of the four states of consciousness: waking, sleeping, dreamless sleep and super-consciousness; of the threefold nature of things and acts: the *satvik* (pure), *rajasik* (active) and *tamasik* (stolid); of the mystic syllable *"Om"* as the most reliable vehicle to achieve God-consciousness. Of *Om* says the Maitreyi Upanishad: "Even as a spider reaches the liberty of space by means of its own thread, the man of contemplation by means of *Om* reaches freedom ... God is sound and silence. His name is *Om.*"

What is remarkable about the Upanishads is the refusal to accept either myth or dogma as creed and instead exhorting people to strive and search for Reality for themselves. This is summed up in the prayer in the *Brihad Aranyaka* which is one of the oldest and longest of Upanishads:

Lead me from delusion to truth
Lead me from darkness to light
Lead me from death to immortality.

It may be mentioned in passing that it was the *Brihad Aranyaka* which inspired the concluding lines of T.S. Eliot's *The Waste Land.* God is within us, says the Upanishad. If you realise your inner self, you realise God. You can realise your inner self by hearing words of divine wisdom, by reflecting and then meditating upon them. You then banish the delusion of duality because then you understand that the worshipper (i.e., yourself) and the object of his worship (i.e., God) are identical. You overcome death. The message comes through clearly in the concluding lines of *The Waste Land* when the clouds thunder Da – *Damyata* (Control yourself); Da – *Datta* (Give in charity); Da – *Dayadhvam* (Be compassionate).

The progress from the Vedas to the Upanishads is from man's concern with external nature to his inner self; from a belief in many gods to a belief in one Supreme Deity. The quest is *atmavidya*, knowledge of the self; the goal is *brahman-atman*, the two names for truth, the two being one and the same.

Sri Ramakrishna illustrated this through a fable. A tiger cub whose mother died giving birth to it was brought up by a herd of goats. It learnt to nibble grass, bleat like them and like them grew to be gentle and harmless. One night a fierce old tiger attacked the flock. The goats ran away; the tiger cub was left with the attacker. It bleated for help and nervously nibbled at a blade of grass. The old tiger took the cub by the scruff of its neck, dumped it beside a limpid pool of water and ordered it to look at its reflection. Then the old fellow took the cub to its den and made it devour goat's meat. It was only then that the cub realised its true nature and learnt to hunt and roar like a tiger.

3

Hinduism-2

The Epics and the Bhagvad Gita

The Vedas and the Upanishads are believed by Hindus to have been revealed (sruti) by God. The Upanishads are in addition regarded as the consummation of Vedic philosophy and therefore described as *Vedanta* – the end, or the *summum bonum* of Vedic knowledge.

As important as the *srutis* are the traditions known as the *Smritis* or the Puranas, meaning old. There are two Puranas, the Mahabharata and the Ramayana.

The Mahabharata is the older and the more voluminous of the two epics; it is, in fact, the longest religious epic of he world, running into as many as 2,009 chapters. In bulk it is eight times as great as that of the *Iliad* and the *Odyssey* put together, and three and a half times that of the entire Bible. The Bhagvad Gita, Song of the Lord, is a part of the Mahabharata. The authorship of this mammoth work is ascribed to the sage Vyasa. But it is quite obvious that it must have taken a generation of writers to compose, compile and polish this epic. It was written sometime between 400 BC and AD 200.

The Mahabharata consists of large number of stories which have been retold, rewritten, and reinterpreted over the centuries. Some like *Shakuntala, Savitri* and *Nala-Damyanti* are as familiar to Hindu children as Hans Andersen's stories are to European or American children. We shall, however, confine ourselves to that part of the story of the Mahabharata which is relative to the Bhagvad Gita.

Mahabharata

The Mahabharata, as we have had occasion to notice before, was written at the time when the Aryans were establishing themselves in northern India. The epic deals with wars between different Aryan tribes, notably the fortunes of the most powerful clan known as the Bharatas.

There was a Bharata king who had two sons. The elder, Dhritarashtra, being blind, gave up his right to the throne to his younger brother Pandu. Dhritarashtra's blindness did not handicap him in other pursuits, for he proceeded to sire a hundred sons known as the Kauravas. His brother Pandu was comparatively abstemious. His first wife, Kunti, bore him only three sons – Yudhishthira was pious, wise and gentle; Bhima was tough, thickheaded and had a gargantuan appetite; Arjuna was noble, generous and brave. Madri, the second wife, bore him two others, Nakula and Sahadeva, good but not as distinguished as their elder brothers.

All went well as long as Pandu lived. On his death Duryodhana, the eldest of Dhritarashtra's hundred sons, burnt down the Pandavas' palace and forced his cousins to flee into the wilderness. Pandu's five sons lived many years in the forests looking after their widowed mother Kunti. They hunted, studied the sacred texts and bided their time to settle scores with the Kauravas.

The Mahabharata is full of stories within stories, each conveying some moral lesson. A good example is an episode that took place during the period of exile. One day Nakula, while hunting, found himself near a pond. He was very thirsty. Just as he was about to go down on his knees to take a palmful of water, he heard a voice say, "Answer my questions before you drink!" It was a crane. Nakula ignored the crane. But no sooner did his lips touch the water than he collapsed and died. One after another, three of his brothers came to the pond. They refused to answer the crane's questions, drank the water and were dead. At last came Yudhishthira, the eldest and the wisest. He paid heed to the crane's warning and agreed to answer its questions.

"What is the road to heaven?" asked the bird.

"Truthfulness," replied Yudhishthira truthfully.

"How does one find happiness?" demanded the crane.

"Through right conduct," replied Yudhishthira.

"What must be subdued in order to escape grief?"

"The mind must be subdued," replied the Pandava.

"When is a man loved?" asked the bird.

"When he is without vanity," came the answer.

"Of all the world's wonders, which is the most wonderful phenomenon?"

Yudhishthira replied, "No man, though he sees others dying all around him, believes that he himself will die. This is the most wonderful phenomenon in the world."

"How does one teach true religion?" asked the crane finally.

"Not by argument, not by scripture or doctrine," replied the wise Yudhishthira. "The true path of religion is the path trodden by saints."

The crane was satisfied and restored life to the dead Pandavas.

The Pandavas' confrontation with the Kauravas took place over Draupadi, the beautiful daughter of another Aryan nobleman. As was the custom, when

Draupadi came of age, her father invited her suitors to take part in a contest of archery. The first was a trial of strength – to string a massive *Gandiva* (bow); then of skill – to shoot the eye of a fish stuck on a mast, by looking at its reflection in a mirror. The Kauravas turned up in their hundred; the five Pandavas emerged from their forest hideout. Other suitors also assembled and the nuptial contest known as a *Swayamvara* began. Only Arjuna was able to string the *Gandiva* and shoot the fish through the eye.

The five brothers triumphantly returned to their jungle hermitage with the comely Draupadi with them. "Mama, see what we have brought with us!" they shouted as they came home. Their mother, Kunti, being busy with domestic work, replied with motherly unconcern, "I am busy, be good boys and share it equally amongst you." The Pandavas did exactly as their mother had told them; they took Draupadi as their common wife.

The Kauravas, needless to say, were very chagrined. They were also concerned about their cousins' claim to half the kingdom. To settle all the issues, they invited the Pandavas to a gambling match.

The Pandavas accepted the challenge. The Kauravas were cunning enough to acquire the services of a wily gambler, Shakuni, their maternal uncle. The Pandavas lost; first their kingdom, then their wife Draupadi and finally themselves. To humiliate the Pandavas further, Dushshasana, one of the Kauravas, dragged her by her

hair into the royal court in session and then tried to
disrobe her by divesting her of her *sari*. However, he
pulled off *sari* after *sari* and yet Draupadi still had a *sari*
on! This miracle was the doing of Lord Krishna, whom
she had implored to save her honour, who kept on
supplying her the garment endlessly. Besides being an
incarnation of God Vishnu, Krishna was also a kinsman
of the Pandavas. The blind Dhritarashtra stopped the
striptease and restored Draupadi to her rightful husbands.
The Pandavas, as they had agreed prior to the gambling
match, went into a thirteen year exile.

When the thirteen years were over, they came
back and again laid
claim to their
inheritance. Once
again the Kauravas
turned it down. This
time the Pandavas
decided to fight it out.
The two armies met
at Kurukshetra, a
town about 80 miles
north-west of Delhi.
Before the battle was
joined, Krishna, now

Krishna-Arjuna

the charioteer to Arjuna, propounded a sermon on the
war of righteousness. This sermon was inserted as a
chapter, the most important chapter, in the
Mahabharata.

Let us get on with the story before we revert to the sermons of the Bhagvad Gita.

The battle of Kurukshetra lasted eighteen days, ended in total defeat for the Kauravas. The Pandavas who returned to rule over the kingdom lived happily ever after, i.e. thirty-six years, with their common wife, Draupadi. Then, like good Hindus, they decided to renounce the world and take the road to Heaven which lay beyond and above the Himalayas. Four brothers and Draupadi died during the journey. Yudhishthira, accompanied by a stray dog which followed him throughout the journey, (who was actually the god Dharma in disguise), arrived at the gates of Indra's paradise. The end will warm the hearts of animal lovers. "No dogs allowed in paradise!" said Indra. "In that case," replied Yudhishthira, "I'd rather not come into your paradise and go instead to hell." Indra's heart was touched: he let in Yudhishthira with his dog. He also reanimated the deceased brothers and their wife to be reunited so that they could live happily in the life hereafter.

The Mahabharata, apart from the Gita, has its philosophical chapter, the *Shantiparva*. What comes through clearly in its stories, aphorisms, parables and sermons is the emphasis on the fourfold aim of life, the four stages of life and the four divisions of society. Life should have four aims: *dharma* (law), *artha* (wealth), *kama* (pleasure) and *moksha* (salvation). A man should divide his life-span into four stages:

Brahmacharya – when he should study and be celibate; *Garhastya* – when he should marry, have a family and earn; *Vanaprastha* – when he should go into the seclusion of a forest and prepare for the last stage; and *Sanyas*, total renunciation of worldly interests. The Mahabharata also assumes the division of society into four castes with which we shall deal later.

The Bhagvad Gita

The Bhagvad Gita is the most important work on the Hindu religion; it is the culmination of the teaching of the Vedas and the Upanishads, "the most exalted of India's religious poems" (Basham); it is the Bible of modern Hinduism. It is the mainspring of the renaissance of Hinduism today: all over the country there is a proliferation of *Gita Pracharini Sabhas*, to propagate the teachings of the Gita. Gandhi acknowledged it as his spiritual reference book. He wrote, "When doubts haunt me, when disappointments stare me in the face, and I see not one ray of hope on the horizon, I turn to the Bhagvad Gita and find a verse to comfort me; and I immediately begin to smile in the midst of overwhelming sorrow." (*Young India*, 6 August 1925.)

The Gita has inspired much religious and secular writing. Its echoes can be heard in the songs of the Sikh Gurus, notably in the haunting melancholy of the compositions of the ninth Guru, Tegh Bahadur. Its spirit is summarised in Kipling's famous poem, "If";

and it was the basis of Aldous Huxley's *The Perennial Philosophy.*

We are still not sure when exactly the Gita was composed. But from the fact that it has no reference to Buddhism, it can be deduced that it is pre-Buddhist. Its language is also of the style of the older passages of the Mahabharata. Scholars, therefore, believe it must have been written some time around 500 BC. Like the rest of the Mahabharata, its authorship is ascribed to the sage Vyasa.

We are not quite sure why the Gita has been incorporated in the Mahabharata, nor of the symbolism (if indeed there is any symbolism at all) in the fact that the Mahabharata consists of eighteen books, the Gita has eighteen chapters and the battle of Kurukshetra lasted eighteen days. It is likely that this philosophic work was inserted in a popular epic to ensure wide readership, to give its philosophic kernel a fictional sugar-coating. It is often described as the inner shrine of the vast temple of the Mahabharata.

A few words about Krishna, the god-philosopher of the Bhagvad Gita, will not be out of place. We do not know his date of birth, but we are sure that he was born at Mathura, a town ninety miles south of Delhi on the right bank of the river Jumna. His parents, Vasudev and Devaki, belonged to a clan of cattle breeders, the Yadavas. Devaki's brother, Kamsa, ruled over the domain. A soothsayer warned Kamsa that Devaki's eighth child would kill him. So Kamsa saw to it that Devaki's children were slain as soon as they were born. The grief-stricken parents were however able to conceal the birth of their eight child, Krishna. The boy was sent across the river to Gokul where he was brought up by a cowherd, Nanda, and his wife, Yashoda.

Krishna grew to be a dark, handsome lad given to pranks. He burst women's pitchers with his catapult, stole their clothes while they were bathing in the river. He was a great flute-player and, like Orpheus, could charm human beings as well as animals. He consumed large quantities of milk and butter and was very strong. He killed many demons including his wicked uncle Kamsa and at one time held up a mountain on his little finger to shelter herds from a torrential downpour. He also had a prodigious appetite for women: he was said to have had 16,000 wives and sired 180,000 sons. His favourite, however, was the milkmaid, Radha – the wife of another cowherd.

Krishna fought many wars against evil-doers. Later in life he married Rukmini, daughter of the King of Vidarbha (Berar) and settled down in Gujarat. He met his end at the hands of a hunter who mistook him for a deer and shot him in the heel.

Krishna is the most popular character of Indian literature, music and painting. The erotic symbolism has its spiritual *double entendre*. Krishna is God; his sweethearts, the *gopis* (chiefly Radha), symbolise the human being's yearning for physical and spiritual fulfilment through union with God. Krishna became the eighth reincarnation of Vishnu.

Let us return to the sermon of the Bhagvad Gita. You will recall the occasion when it is said to have been delivered. The armies of the Kauravas and the Pandavas face each other. It opens with an offer by Krishna to restore King Dhiritarashtra's sight so he can watch the battle. The grief-stricken King replies, "If it is to see my sons, nephews and other kinsmen engaged in killing each other that you will restore light to my eyes, then I would rather stay blind."

A similar grief weighed on the heart of the Pandava, Arjuna. "War, even against evil, is wrong," thinks Arjuna; "It is wrong, because it leads to the destruction of the family which in turn has calamitous consequences on society. Why fight for earthly gains?" he asks.

It will be apparent that Kurukshetra is symbolic of the battle of life. Arjuna is the personification of the thinking man concerned with the ultimate values. His doubts are the doubts of a man pondering over the rights and wrongs of using violence and the goal of human endeavour.

Krishna is the friend, philosopher and guide who provides the answers. The allegory of the chariot, the charioteer and the passenger alluded to in the Upanishads is repeated to illustrate the same theme, viz., the striving of the human soul towards perfection.

Arjuna's dilemma is stated forthwith. He is convinced that his cause is just and the battle he is about to engage in is a *dharmayuddha* – battle for the sake of righteousness. Yet he cannot bring himself to fight his own kith and kin. He is dejected, lets the bow fall from his hand and says firmly, "I will not fight." He knows that it is treason for a commander to make such a statement on the eve of battle. But he is willing to take the consequences of treacherous inaction and defeat, rather than soil his hands with the blood of his kinsmen. Krishna, his charioteer-mentor, answers that only God can take life (which also He has given). Man is only an instrument of His inscrutable design. "He who thinks he slays, he who thinks he is slain, fails to perceive the truth that he neither slays nor is slain." As a mater of fact, says Krishna, there is no death in the sense of a final dissolution because the eternal in man cannot die; it is only a passing from one form to another. Just as a person casts off worn-out clothes and dons new ones, so man when he shakes off this mortal coil – is reborn in some other form. "For one that is born, death is certain; for one who dies, birth is certain," assures Krishna and concludes that man should perform his duty regardless of consequences. "In the hour of trial, strong men should not despair because then they will lose both heaven and earth. They should arise like a fire that burns all before it."

"What, then, is a man's duty?" asks Arjuna.

For a soldier, it is to go to battle when the call to battle comes. All human beings are in a sense soldiers in the battle of life and must likewise perform duties allotted to them. But the performance of this duty should be without consideration for reward (*nishkama karma*). Says Krishna, "Before you go into battle you must learn to treat pleasure and pain, gain and loss, victory and defeat as of no consequence." The same principle holds good in everyday life: to perform tasks allotted to us should be our only right and privilege. We should not look for the fruits of our endeavour. (Recall the last words scribbled in his diary by the Antarctic explorer, Scott, as he lay down to die: "It is the effort that counts, not the applause that follows!")

How can a mortal achieve this state of mental equilibrium in which pleasure and pain, gain and loss, victory and defeat are equally inconsequential? How can one undertake a task with the sole object of performing one's duty without craving for the reward? "Describe a man who is so wise, so steadfast in the performance of his duty. How does he speak, sit, sleep and wake? How do we recognise him?" asks Arjuna.

Krishna replies: When a man puts away all desires out of his mind, when his spirit is content in itself, then he becomes stable in intelligence. He should draw away the senses from the object of the senses as a turtle withdraws its head and legs into its shell. If, on the other hand, a person dwells on the objects of the senses, he inevitably gets attached to those objects. Attachment leads to desire; desire, when frustrated, to anger; anger to bewilderment; bewilderment to loss of memory; loss of memory to destruction of intelligence.

And so does man perish. Those whom the gods wish to destroy, they first make mad.

He into whom desires enter as waters into the sea which, though forever fed by rivers, is not agitated, attains peace. It is a kind of peace which passes understanding. It is like attaining salvation in one's lifetime; one becomes *jeewan-mukta.*

"How does one attain *jeewan-mukti?*" asks Arjuna.

Krishna replies: There are different ways of attaining *jeewan-mukti,* depending on a person's constitution, temperament, inclination and personality. There is the way of knowledge (*gyan-marga*) for men of contemplation; there is the way of action (*karma-marga*) for men of action; and there is the way of love and devotion (*bhakti-marga*).

That may well be so, interposes Arjuna, whose mind now turns to other problems. So often in the world wrong triumphs over right, so often good men suffer while evil men live long, healthy and happy lives. If there is no reward for good, no punishment for evil, why should one bother?

Krishna replies: Whenever righteousness declines and evil is in the ascendant, am I reborn; I am reincarnated as the *Avatar* (Redeemer) to protect the good and destroy evil-doers, to re-establish *Dharma* (the Law). So am I born into this world from age to age. Do not, therefore, worry unduly on this matter as right must ultimately and inevitably triumph over wrong (*satyameva jayate*). I am God, the righter of wrongs, the sustainer of eternal law, *Dharma.* All I ask of you human beings is that you do your duty in the spirit of renunciation.

Renunciation? Queries Arjuna. Does it mean the giving up of everything one has in the world?

No, not that, replies Krishna. It is the unselfish performance of the task allotted; the performance of duty in the spirit of renunciation. This can only be acquired by the practice of yoga.

Krishna then explains the technique of yoga. Shut out all external influences; focus your inner vision between the eyebrows, control your breathing and make the mind one-pointed so as to become oblivious to all desires, anxieties and irritations. In this state of transcendental meditation you will realise that the source of all evil is the ego – *aham-kara* (I-making). But this ego can also be the means of salvation. A man must conquer himself, for "Self alone is the lord of self, self the only means of salvation" – *atta hi attano natho, atta hi attano gatih*.

Krishna further elucidates the essentials of yogic meditation. It does not need great physical stamina or torturing of the flesh. Yoga is not for those who eat too much or eat too little, or sleep too much or sleep too little; one should live a temperate and well-regulated life, seek a quiet place, sit cross-legged on a deer-skin and make the mind one-pointed. The state of one who does achieve this is "like a lamp in a windless place which flickers not". Then is a yogi in union with the Self that is God. To such a one comes the knowledge that God is omniscient, omnipresent, omnipotent – and resides in the hearts of all of us.

"I am the ritual and the sacrifice ... the sacred hymn and offering," says Krishna. "I am seated in the hearts of all creatures; I am the beginning, the middle and the end. Amongst gods, I am Vishnu, of the lights, I am the sun.

"I am God, I accept all manner of homage as equally valid. Whatever form of worship a devotee performs, I make his faith steady ... whosoever offers me with devotion a leaf, a flower, fruit or water, that offering of love from the pure of heart I accept."*

For those who find it difficult to practise the yoga of meditation, Krishna recommends the path of *bhakti* – loving devotion. After this long sermon, Arjuna concedes, "destroyed is my delusion". And proceeds to lead his troops to victory.

Apart from the excellence of the writing, a student should note the following: In the Gita, Vishnu emerges as the Supreme God, the redeemer and preserver of the world. Krishna, who is quite obviously an aboriginal or Dravidian deity, and hence always painted dark and

---

* This sentiment is beautifully echoed in a Tamil folk song:

Into the bosom of the one great sea
Flow streams that come from hills on every side
Their names are various as their springs
And thus in every land do men bow down
To one great God, though known by many names.

normally an amorous, amoral pastoral god, is reincarnated as Vishnu.

The *avatar*, or the redeemer aspect of God, is more precisely emphasised. The *avatar* becomes the pivotal figure in all religions of the Hindu family – Buddhist, Jain, Sikh and others.

The three ways to *moksha*, or salvation, are spelt out with clarity. Thereafter the threefold paths of knowledge, action and devotion find consistent reference in most Hindu religious systems.

The emphasis on the immortality of the soul and its concomitant, the belief in *karma*, i.e., rebirth in different forms depending on one's actions as a human being, became an essential part of Hindu belief. This is also known as *samsara* – birth, death and rebirth.

The Bhagvad Gita's emphasis on renunciation of the reward motive for action (*nishkama karma*) emerges as the most important part of its message. Sri Ramakrishna, a nineteenth century sage of Bengal, used to say that renunciation was the central theme of the Gita and could be comprehended by repeating the words *"Gita, Gita"* and as a chant till it sounded like *"Tyagi, Tyagi"*, meaning renouncer.

And finally, despite the loftiness of its ethics, the Gita accepted the caste system. Brahmins were expected to be serene, pure, disciplined; Kshatriyas, vigorous and heroic; Vaishyas, honest in their dealings; Sudras, hard-working. And the untouchables? They remained beyond the pale of human society.

4

Hinduism-3

We have already stated in passing that the
Mahabharata has many philosophical asides apart from
Krishna's sermon at Kurukshetra. The *Shantiparva* is
a compendium of aphorisms and parables designed to
bring the ethical and philosophical precepts of the
Vedas, the Upanishads and the Gita to the common
people in form and language that they can understand.
The Ramayana, the tale of Rama, has the same object.

The Ramayana was written later and is about a
quarter the size of the Mahabharata. There are many
versions of the epic. The oldest is ascribed to the sage
Valmiki, by caste an untouchable.

The story is briefly as follows:

Once upon a time there was a king named
Dasharatha who ruled over Ayodhya. He had three

wives who bore him four sons, Rama, Bharat, Lakshmana and Shatrughan. They were a very happy and united family, save for Queen Kaikeyi, the mother of Bharat, who wanted her son to succeed his father as the King of Ayodhya.

The neighbouring kingdom was ruled by King Janaka who had a very beautiful daughter named Sita. When Sita was old enough to marry, her father invited all the eligible princes of the country to a *swayamvara*, which took the form of a contest in archery. Rama won the hand of Sita and brought her to Ayodhya. Sita was as dutiful, humble and chaste a girl as Rama was brave, honest and noble. There was no doubt in anyone's mind that they would, in due course, become king and queen of Ayodhya.

Hearing this good news, Queen Kaikeyi became happy, for she loved Rama no less than her own son Bharat. However, her wicked, hunchbacked maidservant, Manthara, soon arrived and worked on her mind, warning her that if Rama became king, she and her son would be relegated to a position of utter unimportance and humiliation. Thereupon, Kaikeyi became alarmed and jealousy and fear possessed her, making her near mad with wild fury. When King Dasharatha entered her apartments, she sat motionless with anger and would not even open her mouth. At last the king promised to remove the cause of her sorrow. Then, as tutored by Manthara, she reminded Dasharatha of the two boons he had given her when she had saved him in the battle of the gods and the demons, when he lay tormented by arrows. That day being the day on which Rama was to be crowned king, Dasharatha begged his queen to put off the question of the boons until after the coronation was over, which she refused. On being told to state her wishes, Kaikeyi asked that her son Bharat be installed forthwith on the throne of Ayodhya and that Rama be banished for fourteen years to the Dandaka forest.

Dasharatha was heartbroken. But the pious Rama insisted on fulfilling his father's pledge. Consequently he, his wife Sita and the younger brother Lakshmana went into the wilderness. Bharat refused to occupy the seat meant for his elder brother. He placed Rama's sandals on the throne and administered Ayodhya in his name.

Rama, Sita and Lakshmana had many adventures as they journeyed through the forests. At one stage, Ravana, the King of Sri Lanka who had heard of Sita's great beauty, disguised himself as a mendicant and when Rama and Lakshmana were out hunting, kidnapped Sita and took her to his island kingdom. Rama and Lakshmana went in pursuit. They raised an army of monkeys under the monkey commander Hanuman and invaded Sri Lanka. They set fire to Lanka, slew Ravana and his brothers and rescued Sita. In due course Sita bore Rama two sons, Lava and Kush.

When the period of exile was over, Rama returned to Ayodhya. There was great rejoicing. Bharat escorted his brother to his throne.

Rama's kingship was marred by vicious gossip about what had transpired when Sita was in exile and abducted by Ravana. The ever-chaste Sita realised the sovereign principle that a king's wife must be above suspicion. She prayed to mother earth to take her back in her womb. The earth split and Sita vanished in it.

For the Hindu, every episode of this story is charged with meaning. Every autumn it is enacted as a passion play in towns, villages and cities. To the Hindu, Rama is the paradigm of all that is noble in a man as Sita is of all that is beautiful and virtuous in a woman. *Ram Rajya*, the age of Rama, is the golden age of a Hindu's dreams and visions; in fact, the name of Rama is a synonym for God. He is the seventh incarnation of Vishnu. He is invoked along with Krishna in the prayers of the Hindus. The revivalists of the Society of Krishna Consciousness use the two gods' names in their litany: "Hare Rama, Hare Krishna." It was with the name of Rama on his lips that Gandhi died.

Since the object of the Mahabharata and the Ramayana was to popularise the philosophical aspects of Vedic Upanishadic-Gitaic Hinduism by putting these precepts in a form and language which the man in the street and the peasant in the field could understand, it is legitimate to conjecture what the common man distilled from the religious and pseudo-religious literature to which he was exposed.

He must have grudgingly conceded that there was, or should really be, one God. But he felt more relaxed with the concept of God as the *Trimurti* – the Creator, Preserver and Destroyer. Despite lip-worship to the idea of one God, he refused to abandon the notion that God or gods reincarnated themselves

Trimurti

as well as their many consorts. The phenomenon of the *avatar* must have had a very strong appeal to a people whose homes and temples were regularly pillaged and razed to the ground by invaders. A poor, oppressed people incapable of rising against their oppressors always pin their hopes on a Redeemer.

No one seriously questioned the caste system. It was predestined. Perhaps it was the operation of the scheme of rewards and punishments for acts done in previous lives. Cosmic law (*samsara*) made good sense. So did *karma*; you reap as you sow. And, of course, what nobler goal than striving for *moksha* (salvation)? Only human beings could hope to discipline themselves to renounce thoughts of worldly acclaim or reward, learn to be detached and conquer their egos and having done so, avoid falling in the snare of the six deadly sins: *kama* (lust), *krodha* (anger), *mad* (pride), *matsarya* (hatred), *moha* (attachment) and *lobha* (greed).

Few, of course, took renunciation to the extreme of asceticism. Most were happy with the religious discipline for the householder, *grihastha dharma*, because the sacred books did allow the pursuit of four objects: *dharma* (law), *artha* (wealth), *kama* (desire) and *moksha* (salvation).

The Caste System

Caste, though sanctioned by scriptural text was, and is, more a sociological than a religious phenomenon.

The origin of the caste system can be traced to the confrontation of the races: the white-skinned, blond and blue-eyed Caucasian with the dark-skinned Dravidian and the yet darker-skinned, negroid adivasis (aboriginals). The word for caste is *varna*, meaning colour.

All societies have caste systems of their own. Before they came to India, the Aryans had their own divisions into the Kshatriyas (nobility) and Vaishyas (commoners). When they subdued the Dravidians, sometime between 3000 and 2000 BC, a third caste came into being, i.e., the conquered people, known as the Dasas or slaves. So it continued for some centuries till the mingling of the races began to cause alarm to the "purists" among the Aryans. And the caste system slowly evolved, dividing society into four groups: the Brahmins (possessed of Brahman, i.e., God) became scholars and priests; Kshatriyas – warriors, enjoying equal status with the Brahmins on account of the political power they wielded and because they were *rajanya* (rulers); Vaishyas, the commoners became the tradesmen; the Sudras, a word whose etymology is unknown but is often presumed to be the name of some non-Aryan tribe, became the workers, artisans, tillers of the soil and rearers of cattle. Then there were those beyond the pale of caste and society, the untouchables, whose only right was to perform the most unpleasant tasks: cleaning lavatories, carrying night soil, skinning carcasses and making footwear.

It should be noticed that the castes represented shades of racial purity as well as functional divisions. A passage in the Mahabharata reads: "Brahmins are fair, Kshatriyas are reddish, Vaishyas are yellowish, Sudras are black." The first three castes came to be known as *dvijas* (the twice-born) and are the only ones entitled to wear the sacred thread (*janeu*), a piece of string worn next to the skin, and read the Vedas.

In the earlier centuries of its development, there was considerable mobility between the four castes. Later it came to be crystallised and the sole criterion became the caste of the parents. The great apologist of the caste-system with whose name it is always linked was the philosopher Manu (circa 600 BC), the author of the *Dharma Shastra* (Book of Sacred Law). He was a Brahmin. This will explain the following observation made by him. "The Brahmin is the lord of all castes ... for the sake of prosperity of the worlds, God caused them to proceed from his mouth, arms (Kshatriyas), thighs (Vaishyas), and feet (Sudras)."

Manu had many things to say on a variety of topics. He denigrated women and prescribed stringent laws with dire punishment for their transgression. Amongst his many pronouncements were rules for students. They had to be celibate. But deviation from the path of celibacy was not so heinous an offence as criticism of the teacher: in his next birth, the student-critic would be born as ass or a dog or a worm, depending on the gravity of his offence against the guru.

It should be borne in mind that the fourfold division is not the most important aspect of the caste system. It is the further subdivision into thousands of sub-castes (*gotras*) which really matters. Caste differences are largely invoked while arranging marriages and eating together: in marriages to keep the progeny "pure"; while eating to ensure that the presence of a lower-caste person does not pollute the food.

Despite many attempts by many reformers to break its shackles, caste concepts have continued to permeate Indian society – Hindu, Muslim, Christian and Sikh. More important than all this is to bear in mind that the problem of untouchability is of a much more serious nature than the rules prescribed for the four castes. Also bear in mind that the entire caste structure including the casteless untouchable is now in a state of flux. The practice of untouchability has been outlawed by the State. Special privileges are accorded to untouchables, many of whom are now members of the central and state cabinets, ambassadors, senior civil servants, doctors, lawyers – and often intermarry people of higher castes.

Popular Hinduism

The philosophic concepts of the Vedas, the Upanishads and the Gita can hardly be discerned in Hinduism as it is practised today. When we go over the history of the country it will be noticed that during the Muslim and British periods it was the folk religion and the sociological make-up of caste that gave Hinduism its resilience. Confronted with Islam and Christianity, Hinduism evolved two distinct attitudes: the liberal, which emphasised the essential tolerance of Hinduism towards other religions; and an isolationist, chauvinistic, aggressive attitude which equated India with Hindu and rejected other religions not of Indian origin as foreign abominations. The liberal attitude was nurtured by the medieval saints like Chaitanya, Kabir, Nanak and continued by the Brahmo Samaj, the Prarthana Samaj, the Theosophists, the Ramakrishna Mission and manifested itself in the teachings of Sri Aurobindo, Gandhi and agnostics like Nehru and his daughter, Indira Gandhi. Indian secularism is a product of this liberal tradition. The second attitude was expressed in the glorification of warriors who fought the Muslims:

Prithvi Raj Chauhan, Rana Pratap, Shivaji (1627-80) and Guru Gobind Singh (1666-1708) and later in the revivalist movements, chiefly the Arya Samaj of Dayanand Saraswati (1829-83) – and is today the philosophy of the Bharatiya Janata Party (formerly Bharatiya Jan Sangh) and its paramilitary wing, the RSS (Rashtriya Svayamsevak Sangh). The clash between the two opposing attitudes was climaxed in the murder of the liberal Gandhi by Godse, a fanatical member of the RSS.

Let us take a brief glimpse at Hinduism as it is practised today.

The vast majority of Hindus believe in a variety of gods and goddesses – human, animal, floral and phenomenal. The number of *devatas* are said to be over 330 million. Every village has its village deity. On the outskirts of every town and hamlet you will see some banyan or peepul tree with its bole surrounded by stone phalluses and images of snakes, monkeys and such others. Most Hindu homes also have their own family deity in a niche. They will awaken it with the chanting of hymns, lighting joss-sticks, daubing it with vermilion powder; they will festoon it with flowers, offer it food and coconut milk. And at sunset, they will wave salvers full of oil lamps and smoking agar, blow conch-shells, clang bells and then put it to rest.

Of the *Trimurti* – the threefold aspect of God – Brahma, the creator, now receives scant attention. Vishnu, the preserver, is in the ascendant through his many reincarnations, the two most popular being Rama with his wife Sita (along with their monkey general Hanuman) and Krishna with his beloved (not wife) Radha. Vishnu has had ten reincarnations; the last, Kalki, has yet to make his appearance.

Siva, the destroyer, shares Vishnu's popularity. He is not only the destroyer but also the life-force, the king of ascetics as well as the lord of song, dance and occult magic. He is represented in human form with his chignon held by the crescent moon and the Ganges flowing out of his tresses. He wears cobras round his neck and arms. He is also represented symbolically by his phallus or his trident. His consorts – Parvati, Durga, Naina, Bhavani, Jagadamba and Kali – enjoy equal popularity as mother goddesses of destruction and recreation. Siva's son, the elephant-headed Ganesha, is the god of auspicious beginnings, the patron saint of scholars, who decorates the portals of many Hindu homes. Most religious dissertations begin by paying homage to him: *Shri Ganeshaya namah.*

★

Pilgrimages and bathing in holy rivers form an essential part in the life of a devout Hindu. The Ganga is the holiest of all rivers. Along the Ganga are holy cities, Rishikesh, Hardwar, Benares and Prayag (modern Allahabad), where the other holy river, the Jumna, meets it. Here at the *sangam* (confluence of rivers) the

Hardwar

Kumbh Mela takes place every twelve years, when as many as two million people are known to take a ritual dip in its turgid waters. There are other sacred rivers like the Narmada and the Godavari with their own holy cities and special days for ritual bathing.

India is littered with places of pilgrimage (*teerthasthanas*). In the north there are Kurukshetra, Mathura, Brindavan, Hardwar, Benares and Jagannath Puri. In Central India there are Pandharpur and Nasik. In the south, there are Madurai, Tirupathi, Trivandrum and a host of others.

Hindu festivals are too numerous to enumerate. There is a popular Hindi saying, *sat var aur ath tyohar;* "A week has seven days and eight religious festivals." The more important are: *Dussehra* (commemorating

Rama's return from exile); *Divali,* the festival of lamps: *Holi,* the water festival marking the end of winter; *Janmashtami,* the birth anniversary of Krishna. Maharashtra has its *Ganapati* and *Sivaratri* (the night of Siva); the South of India its *Onam.*

Reverence for the Brahmin is on the decline. He has been reduced to the status of a priest or a cook. But he has succeeded in reincarnating himself as a *swami* – yogi or sadhu; most of this fraternity are Brahmins. The religious teacher is much in vogue. He may have his own *ashrama* or *math* with a circle of disciples; he may fly around in planes and address large meetings over the microphone. Having European and American disciples adds to his prestige. People in their thousands seek him out for spiritual solace.

Palmistry and astrology are also as deeply embedded in the Hindu mind as ever before. Western education, scientific advancement and sophistication have barely affected the Hindu's predilection to look to the stars and the lines on the palms of his hand for guidance. Horoscopes must be "matched" before matches are made; auspicious days must be awaited before any important move is made. Even card-holding communists are known to wait for auspicious days to file nomination papers in elections. Wearing of charms, amulets and lucky stones in rings is a common practice. In 1963 when eight planets were in "fatal" conjunction, spelling the doom of the world, Hindus propitiated their gods by burning tons of ghee (clarified butter) in sacrificial fires. People in high places, like ministers, generals, secretaries and heads of departments, are known to consult astrologers regularly.

In his lifetime a Hindu male will undergo many religious ceremonies. The first will be the naming (*namkaran samskara*), followed by the shaving of the head (*mundan*) when all the hair of the head, save a tuft, will be shaved off. If he belongs to one of the upper three castes, he will be invested with a sacred thread (*yagya upavitam*). When he is old enough – between sixteen and twenty – he will be married. Many religious rituals precede the nuptials, but the essential one is circling the sacrificial fire seven times with the bride trailing behind him. When he dies he will be cremated, his ashes scattered in a river, preferably the Ganges. His close kinsmen will shave their heads, his widow discard all her jewellery and forgo wearing vermilion powder in the parting of her hair. Thereafter, every year his relatives will observe obsequial ceremonies (*shraddha*) by feeding Brahmins and having them say prayers for his soul.

5

Jainism and Buddhism

*T*here are not many Jains or Buddhists in India. The few that are, are reckoned as Hindus. Their importance is historical in as much as they represented movements protesting against Brahmanical Hinduism and moulded later Hindu thought.

Jainism

The word "Jain" is derived from Jina, the conqueror, or the victor, i.e., one who has conquered himself. The Jains believe that their religious system was evolved by twenty-four *tirthankaras* (ford-finders *or makers of the river crossing*), three of whom, Rhishabha, Ajitnath and Aristanemi systematised their religious doctrines. Most of Jain hagiography is legendary. But we do have reliable historical evidence of the existence of Parasvanath (872-772 BC), the 23rd *tirthankar*, and the 24th, Mahavira (599-527 BC). There is reason to believe that in its formative phase Jainism was a reaction against Brahmanical Hinduism. Jainism had also drawn inspiration from some other religious system,

Mahavira

probably Zoroastrianism, which at the time flourished in Persia. A recurring feature of Jain legends is the continuous struggle from one generation to the other between good and evil, the fratricidal feud between Cain and Abel, the battle between the forces of light and the forces of darkness. The conflict between *Ahura Mazda* and *Angra Mainyu* was also the central theme of the teachings of Zoroaster. The Zoroastrian representation of Satan with serpents rising on his shoulders also recurs in Jain iconography.

Though Jain scholars trace the origin of their faith to the Vedic period, most people look upon Mahavira as the founder of Jainism.

Vardhamana Mahavira (increasing-great-warrior) was born in 599 BC in Kundagrama, a town north of Patna. He was the second son of a nobleman and was reared in the lap of luxury. The Jains love to enumerate everything. According to them the child Mahavira was cared for by five nurses and enjoyed five kinds of joy. When he came of age he was married and his wife bore him a daughter. But neither his wife nor his child, nor affairs of state occupied his mind. On the death of his parents (according to one version, by suicide), he took permission of his elder brother to retire to the jungles. He was then thirty years old. For twelve years he fasted and meditated "in a squatting position, with joined heels, exposing himself to the heat of the sun, with knees high and the head low, in deep meditation". In the midst of abstract meditation, he reached *kevala* (total) omniscience. He became *nirgrantha* – without ties or knots.

Mahavira discarded his clothes and spent the next thirty years of his life wandering from place to place. He spoke to no one, never stayed anywhere more than one night, ate only raw food and strained the water he drank. He allowed vermin to feed on his body and carried a broom to sweep insects away from his path lest he trod on them. People scoffed at him and often tormented him. But he never said anything to them. He died in 527 BC or, as the Jains put it, at the age of seventy-two, "he cut asunder ties of birth, old age and death".

Mahavira, like his Jain predecessors, was given to neatly compartmentalising subjects and enumerating them. Here are some instances of the Jain predilection to itemising. There are nine kinds of meritorious actions;

eighteen kinds of sinful actions; eighty-two ways in which the *jiva* (life-force) pays the penalty for sinful actions. Knowledge, said Mahavira, is of five kinds: cognitive (*mati*), symbolic (*sruti*), clairvoyant (*arudhi*), telepathic (*manahpraya*) and perfect, i.e., all embracing (*kevala*). We need not analyse his theory of knowledge. More important from the religious point of view was his theory of the life-force (*jiva*).

Everything, animate or inanimate, has *jiva*, said Mahavira. Plants, fire, wind, water, earth, all have life. The worst thing a human being can do is to take *jiva*. "He who lights fire kills living beings; he who puts it out kills the fire," says a Jain text with relentless logic. This is the extreme example of Jain hylozoism.

Karma or actions are of fifty-seven kinds. They partake of the nature of particles which flow into the *jiva* and, as particles of uric acid accumulate and foul the body with arthritis, so do our acts fill our souls as sand fills a bag and weighs it down. The *jiva*, or the soul, is more like a bubble or a balloon with a buoyant, upward-moving tendency; it is its *karma* which weighs it down. *Karma* not only determines the form of our worldly existence but also keeps us entangled in the wheel of births, deaths and rebirths. The goal of human endeavour should be to exhaust *karma* by first plugging its inflow (*samsara*) and then dissipating what is left (*nirjara*) by ascetic penance (*tapas*) till the very seed (*karma bija*) is burnt up.

Jainism is not a passive religion; it recommends exertion (*kriya*) so that the "crystallised particles of the soul's past experiences and unfulfilled desires" are purged. "Man, thou art thy own friend; why seekest thou a friend beyond thyself?" asks a Jain text. "The soul is the maker and the non-maker. It itself makes happiness and misery, decides its own condition, good or evil, it is its *Vaitarani* – the river of torment in hell. This is known as the doctrine of *Kriyavada* (self).

The way of deliverance, said Mahavira, is in the pursuit of three gems (*tri-ratnas*), or rules of conduct; (i) Right faith (ii) Right knowledge and (iii) Right conduct.

Right conduct prescribes the following five principles:

(i) Sanctity of life (*ahimsa paramo dharma* – non-violence is the supreme law)
(ii) Truthfulness
(iii) Respect for property
(iv) Chastity
(v) Abandonment of worldly possessions.

A Jain, when he becomes a monk, takes the following vow: "I shall become a *sramana* who owns no house, no property, no sons, no cattle. I shall eat what others give me. I shall commit no sinful act."

In this way life on this earth and the life-hereafter become a purgatory of *karma*, and the *jiva* is absorbed in the *Paramatman*. It is like "the melting of a dew drop into the silent sea". The absorption in the *Paramatman* is the goal of Jain endeavour. The Jain's heaven is a safe, happy, quiet place where there is no ageing, no pain, no disease or death.

God has no place in Jain theology. Instead, Jains believe in "enlightened" human beings because escape is only possible in human form. Jains also reject the Vedas, the priestly order of the Brahmins and the caste system.

Jains were soon divided into two sects – the *svetambaras* (*sveta* – white, *ambara* – clothes) and the *digambaras* ("skyclad", i.e., clad in elements that fill the four corners of the sky). The *digambaras* go naked, do not allow women to join the holy orders and recognise no canon. For obvious climatic reasons the *Svetambaras* survive in the colder climes of northern India; the *Digambaras* thrive in the warmer climate of the south. There is a third Jain sub-sect, the *Sthanakavasis*, who believe neither in idols nor in organised worship: the spirit, they say, is everywhere.

We are not quite certain how large a following the Jains had at different times, but there is ample evidence proving their influence on many thinkers. They gained the patronage of Chandragupta Maurya in the North and the Hoysala dynasty in the South. They were always a rich community and patronised the arts. Their temples are some of the most beautiful in the country. Mount Parasnath, Girnar, Satrunjaya in Palitana, Ranakpur and Dilwara on Mount Abu are some splendid examples of Jain architecture. Jain images differ from those of the Hindus and the Buddhists. "An idol before a worshipper," say the Jains, "is like a flower before a mirror." The mind reflects what is in front of it and takes on its colour. Hence Jain images are "passionless" and alabaster-cool. Says a Jain sage, "Reflect on the reactions of a lecher, a dog and a saint towards the naked corpse of a beautiful woman. The lecher would like to copulate with it, the dog devour it, and the saint pray for its soul. Hence, you must make sure that what you see in your hours of meditation is appropriate to the spirit of meditation."

The renaissance of Hinduism in the Middle Ages and persecution by Saivites took a toll of Jain following. The Jains lost most because of their close affinity to Hinduism and the continuous, frequently one-way, intermarriage with the Hindus. Attempts to organise themselves and retain their separate identity had limited success. In 1893 an All India Digambar Jain Conference was set up. Six years later (1899) a Jain Youngmen's Association was organised which in 1910 became the Bharatiya Jain Mahamandal. Its motto was "*Maitribhava sarvam jayati*" – love conquers all.

Jain influence in India is largely due to the comparative affluence of the Jain community. Some of India's biggest industrial houses are Jain – Dalmias, Sarabhais, Walchands, Kasturbhai, Lalbhais, Sahus, Jains. The proportion of literacy among them is also high. Mahatma Gandhi was greatly influenced by the Jain doctrine of *ahimsa* (non-violence) which he elevated from a personal and ethical creed to a programme of national and political policy.

Buddhism

Buddhism is one of the great religions that India gave to the world. Although discarded, it permeated Indian thinking and is in the process of being regenerated in the land of its birth as neo-Buddhism.

Let us first acquaint ourselves with the events in the Buddha's life as accepted by the Buddhists.

There was a chieftain named Suddhodana, a Kshatriya of the Sakya clan whose domain lay somewhere on the Indo-Nepal frontier of today. One night his queen, Maya, dreamt that a six-tusked elephant had entered her womb. Sooth-sayers pronounced that a son, immaculately conceived would either rule the world or the hearts of the people of he world. In the year 563 BC, while Queen Maya was in her garden at Lumbini

Buddha

holding the branch of an *ashoka* tree, she was delivered of a child from her side. The child was named Siddhartha (he-who-had-realised-his-goal) with the patronymic Gautama by which he is generally known. Later, when he attained spiritual eminence, he came to be referred to as the *Sakyamuni,* the mendicant-scholar of the Sakya clan or, more popularly, as Gautama the Buddha, the wise one.

As the scion of a princely household, Siddharatha had all he desired. His father Suddhodana, however, discerned an otherworldly streak in him and saw to it that the lad was not exposed to the unpleasant realities of the world. He also arranged the boy's marriage to a beautiful cousin, Yasodhara. For a while Yasodhara succeeded in beguiling her husband's time in pursuit of pleasure. She bore him a son, Rahul.

Gautama's mind began to wander beyond the luxuries of his palace walls. One day he rode out on his chariot into the streets. What he saw made him repeat the excursion another three days. On these four outings he saw four sights which made a deep impression on his mind. The first day he saw a tottering old man, the second day a man stricken with disease, the third day a corpse being carried for cremation and on the fourth he encountered an ascetic with a beatific unconcern with the goings-on around him. The moment of truth had come. One night when he was only twenty-nine years of age, Gautama stole out of the palace to seek the answer to the afflictions of the world.

He first went to Rajgriha and studied under two Brahmin scholars. He was not satisfied with their teachings. He then joined a party of five ascetics and for six years, fasted and tortured his body till he was almost dead. Then he renounced asceticism. "This way of mortification has utterly failed me," he said. "My body cannot support my intellect. I will eat and drink and strengthen it ... There must be a middle way between living in luxury and ascetic austerity," he thought to himself. He became a *tathagata*, a truth-finder. He came to Gaya and once more resumed his train of thought. Seated under the traditionally sacred bo tree, he resolved, "Though skin, nerves and bone shall waste away and life-blood itself be dried up, here sit I till I attain enlightenment." In due course, "ignorance was destroyed, darkness dispelled, knowledge had arisen, light had arisen". Said the Buddha, "My task is done." He had attained *nirvana*.

The Buddha travelled westwards till he came to Benares, the holy city of the Hindus. His five erstwhile companions rejoined him. He propounded his theme of the middle path in a deer park at Sarnath, a suburb of Benares. "There are two extremes which he who has given up the world ought to avoid. What are these two extremes? A life given to pleasures and lusts: this is degrading, sensual, vulgar, ignoble, profitless. And a life given to mortification: this is painful, ignoble and profitless. By avoiding these two extremes, the truth-finder (*tathagata*) has gained the knowledge of the middle path which leads to insight, which leads to wisdom, conduces to calm, to knowledge, to enlightenment, to *nirvana*."

He proceeded to tell them of the Four Noble Truths and the Eightfold Path of Discipline. This, in Buddhist terminology, came to be known as setting the wheel of law (*Dharma Chakra*) in motion.

The Buddha's first converts were his five companions. The circle of companions soon widened to sixty, which included two of his cousins, Ananda and Devdutta. Thereafter, many princes and commoners joined the fold.

The Buddha travelled extensively over northern India, preaching the Four Noble Truths and the Eightfold Path and taking part in dialogues with other seekers. He established the Buddhist community – the *Sangha*. After 45 years of his ministry, he died at the age of 80 at Kusinara near Benares. His birth, *nirvana* and *parinirvana* (death) were by coincidence on the same day of the year – the full moonlit night of the harvest moon.

What did the Buddha preach? The Four Noble Truths:

1. There is sorrow and suffering (*dukha*) in the world. This was not, according to the Buddha, among the doctrines handed down to him, but perceived "within me by an eye to perceive". About *dukha*, he said, "The waters of the four great oceans are

less than the tears shed by men in the interminable course of existence for the loss of their dear ones."

2. The cause of that sorrow and suffering is craving (tanha).

3. *Tanha* can be overcome.

4. The way to overcome *tanha* and attain *nirvana* is to follow the Eightfold Path of Righteousness, i.e., to hold right beliefs and aspirations; to be right in speech and conduct; to have right means of livelihood and effort; to be right in mind and in meditation.

The Buddha did not condemn all desires but only those that caused *dukha* (sorrow). The desire to love and hate were undesirable. "Those who love nothing and hate nothing have no fetters," he said. "Those who love a hundred dear ones have a hundred woes; those who have ninety dear ones have ninety woes; those who have one dear one have one woe; those who hold nothing dear have no woe."

The goal of human endeavour, said the Buddha, should be to attain *nirvana* which is not annihilation but release. *Nirvana*, said the Buddha, is "deep, immeasurable, hard to fathom, and like a great ocean". In short, it is indefinable. "Definition is not important", assures the Buddha, "it is achieving which matters ... A wounded person should not ask the physician what kind of arrow hit him or who shot it ... Some ascetics and Brahmins have accused me, baselessly, falsely and groundlessly of being a nihilist preaching annihilation, destruction and non-existence. That is not true. I teach of pain and cessation of pain."

The Buddha rejected the authority of the Vedas and the paths of knowledge (*gyan-marga*) and devotion (*bhakti-marga*), presumably thus accepting the third alternative path, viz., of action (*karma-marga*) The Buddha's was a practical faith. To his son Rahul, the Buddha gave the golden rule of conduct: "When there is a deed you wish to do, then think thus: is it conducive to my own harm or to the harm of others or both? Then it is bad." And he advised his disciples: "Inculcate love (*metta*), endure insults of those that insult you, do not resist, for hatred does not cease by hatred, but hatred ceases by love."

In the parting message to his disciples he exhorted self-reliance. "Be ye lamps unto yourselves ... be ye a refuge unto yourselves. Betake yourselves no external refuge. Hold fast to the truth ..." In the *Dhammapada*, the ultimate message is summed up thus:

> By ourselves is evil done, by ourselves we pain endure;
> By ourselves we cease from wrong, by ourselves become we pure.
> No one saves us but ourselves, no one can and no one may;
> We ourselves must tread the path, Buddhas only show the way.

The Buddha's faith was not speculative, nor metaphysical but pragmatic. In a sermon he said, "I have not elucidated that the world is eternal ... finite ... and that the soul and body are identical ... because it profits not nor has to do with the fundamentals of religion."

The Buddha's concept of *karma* and transmigration was a slight variation of the Brahmanical concept: "*Arhats* (enlightened monks) attain salvation (*jeewan-mukti*) in their lifetime and for them there is no rebirth ... the wise are extinguished at death like a lamp ... but those who die with the desire to live and to possess still sparking in them, will be reborn."

According to the Buddha, ego comprises the body, feeling, cognition, intuition and judgement (*skandha*). At death *skandha* is destroyed. When the disciples protested that if judgement is destroyed at death, then there is nothing left to transmigrate or be reborn, the Buddha replied that transmigration or rebirth is as "one taper is lit from another, as learning is passed from teacher to pupil". The Buddha also rejected the caste system:

> It is not right to call men white who virtue lack,
> For it is sin and not the skin that makes men black,
> Not by the cut of hair, nor by his clan or birth
> May a Brahmin claim the Brahmin's name
> But only by real worth.

After the passing of the Buddha, 500 disciples met at Rajgriha to make a definitive compilation of the

Master's teachings. This was not in Sanskrit which had become a monopoly of the Brahmins but in Pali, the language spoken by the common people. The Pali canon later came to be known as the *Tipitaka*, the Three Baskets. The first is known as the *Vinaya Pitaka*. The second, *Satta Pitaka*, was a compilation of the Buddha's sermons. The third, *Abidhamma Pitaka*, deals with psychological problems.

The monastic order of Buddhists became the nucleus of missionary effort. Dressed in yellow robes, his head shaven, with a begging bowl in hand, the Buddhist monk did his rounds from house to house stopping briefly to make his presence known and accept whatever was put in his bowl. Then he retired into solitude to meditate. The creed of Buddhists became trust in the Buddha, in the sacred law and in the community:

> *Buddham saranam gacchami* – I take refuge in the Buddha.
> *Dhammam saranam gacchami* – I take refuge in the law.
> *Sangham saranam gacchami* – I take refuge in the order.

Ten precepts were laid down for the monks: do not kill, do not steal, remain chaste, do not lie, do not take intoxicants, eat little, do not indulge in pleasures (dance, drama, etc.), do not wear perfume, jewellery, etc., do not sleep on a soft couch, do not accept gifts of gold or silver. (It will be noticed that the first four precepts are exactly the same as those of the Jains. These four applied equally to laymen and to ordained monks.)

Although Buddhism spread very rapidly, its followers split into many factions. Within a century, eighteen different Buddhist sects were recorded. A second council was called, 100 years after the first, at Vedali. It failed to reconcile the different points of view.

Buddhism received its greatest fillip under the Mauryas. Emperor Asoka, after waging a victorious but bloody battle at Kalinga, became an ardent Buddhist (around 273 BC). He had Buddhist precepts spread all over the country inscribed on pillars and cut into rocks. He sent missionaries to neighbouring countries. His own son took the message to Sri Lanka. In the fifth century AD, Buddhaghosa translated the Pali text into Sinhalese and in due course the whole of Sri Lanka accepted Buddhism.

By the first century AD Buddhism had spread through Tibet to China and in another 500 years became the dominant faith in both countries.

For over 800 years after Asoka, Buddhism remained the dominant faith in India. But by AD 1000 it was in full retreat against revivalist Hinduism. Since many of the salient features of Buddhism were taken from Hinduism, they were reabsorbed into Hinduism with their Buddhist overtones. Consequently, when the Muslims invaded India, while Hinduism had the resilience to withstand the Islamic onslaught, Buddhism crumbled and vanished from the country.

We will not go into the various sects of Buddhism, the *Mahayana* (the great vehicle), the Lamaism of Tibet, the Zen Buddhism of Japan, the *Hinayana* (the lesser vehicle) or the *Therravada* of Sri Lanka, Burma, Thailand, for the simple reason that they are not relevant to India.

The teachings of the Buddha left a permanent mark on Indian thought. "Buddhism today lives in the lives of those Indians who have not given up their past traditions ... the Buddha's presence is felt all around." (Radhakrishnan.)

There has been a rebirth of Buddhism in India. The Theosophists revived interest in the faith. The Mahabodhi Society, set up in 1891, and later the Bharatiya Boudh Mahasabha re-spread the message. The windfall came in 1956 with the mass conversions of untouchables (Mahars of Maharashtra and Christians) to Buddhism. Since the Chinese invasion of Tibet, India has acquired a sizeable population of Tibetan Buddhists, including the Buddha's reincarnation, the Dalai Lama. The 1981 census put the figures of Buddhists at 47,19,900.

It may be worth recording that the two national emblems of free India, the Lion Capital and the Chakra are both of Buddhist origin.

6

Islam and Indian Muslims

*M*uslims are India's largest religious minority and form over 12 per cent of the population of the country. Next to Indonesia and Bangladesh, India has the third largest Muslim population in the world. Their position in India is the acid test of India's claims to being a secular state, for not only is Islam (like Christianity, Zoroastrianism and Judaism) outside the mainstream of Hinduism, but before independence the majority of Indian Muslims helped carve out of Indian soil the Muslim State of Pakistan. Most non-Muslims continue to be sceptical of Muslim professions of loyalty to India. These considerations make a close study of Indian Mussulmans of vital importance.

First let us acquaint ourselves with the life of the founder of Islam, Prophet Mohammed, and his teachings. Thereafter, we shall deal with the advent of Islam in India, its impact on Hinduism and its growth in the Indian environment.

In the sixth century AD Mecca was a thriving commercial town with a population of Jews, Christians and idolators. The majority of the Meccans worshipped a meteorite embedded in the Ka'aba, a massive column alongside which were images of Hubal and three goddesses. Meccans were not only divided in worship but also into tribes and clans hostile to each other. The two major tribes were the Quraish and the Khoz'ah. The Quraish were further subdivided into the Hashimites

Mecca

and the Omayyads. As long as business was good, Meccans managed to get along with one another. But early in the century caravans found new routes which bypassed Mecca. As prosperity declined, bitterness among the tribes increased. Meccans developed all the evils of a decadent society: beggary, prostitution, drink, gambling and violence.

In the year AD 570, Mohammed of the Hashimite branch of the Quraish was born. He was a posthumous child orphaned by the death of his mother when he was only six. He was brought up by his grandfather and later his uncle, Abu Talib.

Travelling with the caravans of his uncle, young Mohammed saw other Arab lands like Syria and Palestine. He took employment as a camel-driver with a wealthy widow, Khadijah, and later married the lady, fifteen years older than himself. As long as she lived he took no other wife. She bore him two sons, both of whom died in infancy, and three daughters. One of the daughters, Ruqqayah, married Osman (who later became the third caliph) and Fatima, the only child to survive him, married his own cousin Ali, the son of his uncle Abu Talib. Ali became the fourth caliph and the father of the Prophet's grandsons, Hassan and Hussain.

The call to found a new religion came to Mohammed when he was in the employment of Khadijah. While grazing her flocks, he was wont to retire into the solitude of a cave on Mount Hira. There one afternoon the archangel Gabriel appeared before him and commanded him to recite. Mohammed did as he was told. And the voice of God spoke through him. The first utterance (the 46th *sura* of the Quran) was as follows:

> In the name of thy Lord who created
> Man of a blood-clot, Recite!
> "And thy Lord is the most generous,
> Who taught by the pen.

Taught man that he knew not.
No indeed; surely man waxes insolent,
For he thinks himself self-sufficient.
Surely unto thy Lord is the returning."

The experience was repeated a few days later. Mohammed told his wife what had passed with him. Without hesitation she acknowledged him as the new prophet (*nabi*) and apostle (*rasul*) of Islam (submission-to-God). Thereafter, his cousin Ali, then his slave, and then two kinsmen, Abu Bakr and Osman, became Muslims.

Mohammed's proclamation of Prophecy aroused animosity and derision amongst the Meccans, chiefly among his own tribesmen, the Quraish. In four years, Mohammed was not able to gain even forty followers. In these four years his rich wife Khadijah and his uncle Abu Talib died. After their deaths Mohammed was more than ever before exposed to the hostility of the Meccans. His name had, however, spread amongst the wandering Bedouin and people in distant Medina heard of his reputation as a divinely inspired orator and a man of God. The Medinese invited him to migrate to their city.

In AD 622, Mohammed fled Mecca and went to Medina. The *Hejira*, or the flight, is the first most important date in the Muslim calendar. Thereafter Muslims began to reckon events from the *hijri*.

It was in Medina that Mohammed raised the first mosque (*masjid*). The first call to prayer (*azan*) was heard from its minaret and the first prayers for Muslims (*namaz*) were formulated.

The Meccans tried to seize Mohammed. The attempts were repulsed. Soon, Mohammed claimed a following strong enough to turn the tables on his persecutors. He captured Mecca and demolished the idols in the Ka'aba. Mohammed, however, allowed the worship of the meteorite to continue, took over the ancient ritual and made it a part of Islamic tradition.

Mohammed died in AD 632. He was succeeded as Viceroy (Khalifah) by Abu Bakr. Abu Bakr was followed in succession by Omar, Osman and Ali. The order of succession was disputed and schisms in Islam began. We shall discuss them later.

Mohammed has been much vilified by many scholars. Amongst the most villainous denigrators were Dante and Carlisle. In the India of recent times, the chief critic was Swami Dayanand Saraswati, the founder of the Arya Samaj which led the renaissance of Hinduism in India in the nineteenth century. (The Swami was equally intemperate in his criticism of Jesus Christ and other prophets, including the gurus of the sikhs.) It is this kind of ill-informed and vituperative denigration of a man whom Muslims revere as the most perfect man ever born, that makes Muslims adopt defensively aggressive postures against other religious systems. The Muslims' reverence for the Quran, the word of God spoken through Mohammed, is also a unique phenomenon. It has fired millions of Muslims

with a degree of religious
fervour unknown to followers
of other religious systems.

What did Mohammed
teach? A summary of his
teachings is in the five pillars
(*arakan*) of Islam.

First, the creed (*iman*):
there is no God save Allah
and Mohammed is His
Messenger. The Muslims
revere other prophets like

The Quran

Abraham, Moses and Jesus but none that claim to
have come after Mohammed. Mohammed put the final
seal on prophecy; he was the *khatm-un-nabi*, the last
of the prophets.

Second, prayer (*salat* in Arabic; in Persian and
Urdu *namaz*). There are five prayers selected from the
114 *suras* (chapters) of the Quran. The prayers were
given final shape during the caliphate of Osman. Five
times during the day and night a Muslim must turn
his face towards Mecca, genuflect and recite his prayers.

Third, the giving of alms (*zakat*).

Fourth, fasting (*rauza*) from sunrise to sunset
during the ninth lunar month, *Ramadan*.

Fifth, pilgrimage (*haj*) to Mecca during the twelfth
lunar month, *Dhu'l Hijja*.

Besides these five pillars there is the code of
conduct (*ihsan*). In the traditions (Hadith) ascribed to

Mohammed there are innumerable injunctions against gambling, drinking, adultery, stealing and other unsocial practices.

Said the Prophet, "There is no piety in turning your faces towards the east or the west, but he is pious who believes in Allah, the Day of Judgement, Angels, the Quran and the prophets; he who for the love of Allah disburses wealth to his kindred, to orphans, to the needy and to travellers."

One point which deserves special attention is the Prophet's attitude towards non-Muslims. "Slay those who ascribe partners to God," says the Quran (*Sura* IX, verse 5). Confrontation with the infidel was *jihad* (holy war). The Prophet specifically excepted Jews and Christians from the taint of infidelity because they were *shi-kitab* (people of the Book, the Torah and the Bible). No such exemption was provided for the Hindu or the Jain or the Buddhist, or for their religious offshoots which came later.

The Spread of Islam

The new religion of Mohammed brought new life to Arabia. Mecca once again became the centre of pilgrimage, the meeting-place for caravans and a busy entrepot. Islam united the warring Arab tribes into one nation. So great was the impetus of this union that within a few years Muslim Arabs spilled over the neighbouring countries, carrying the message of Islam with scimitar and fire in the most spectacular outburst of a people's movement known in history. Within four years of the death of the Prophet AD 636, they took Jerusalem. Within eleven years AD 643, they overran Persia and Egypt. They went right across northern Africa to its Atlantic shores, crossed the straits of Gibraltar into Spain and reached the heart of France till they were held at Tours in AD 732. They also conquered the countries of the Adriatic and captured Constantinople. Savage tribes of Turkistan, Central Asia and China accepted Islam and carried the triumphal flag of Islam through Persia and Afghanistan into India. Arab mariners became the masters of the Mediterranean and the Arabian Seas and the Indian Ocean.

Islam in India

Arab traders were known to the people of the west coast of India, stretching from the mouth of the Indus down to Cape Comorin (Kanyakumari) in the South. When the same traders brought with their old merchandise of dates and frankincense their new faith, the Hindus, as was their wont, heard them with open minds. They allowed the Muslims to raise mosques and make converts. Some Hindus gave their daughters in marriage to the Arabs. Thus colonies of Muslims came to be established on the west coast. One surviving example of these early Arabian-Indian Muslims are the *moplahs* (from "mapilla" meaning "son-in-law") in the state of Kerala.

The peaceful spread of Islam in India stopped when Muslim armies began to invade the country.

The first such invasion took place in AD 712 when the youthful Arab commander, Mohammed Bin Qasim, overran Sindh. There was a lull of two hundred years before the Muslim storm broke over India. In AD 1000 Mahmud of Ghazni went through the Punjab to Delhi and beyond, massacring Hindus, destroying Hindu temples and looting Hindu cities. In a series of seventeen invasions, one of which took him as far as Somnath on the coast of Gujarat, he paved the way for Islam. But it was a bloody path strewn with the debris of Hindu gods and temples and the skeletons of those he had killed. As one would expect, Mahmud's incursions bred hatred in the minds of the Hindus towards everything Muslim. Hindu resistance in northern India was finally overcome by Mohammed Ghori who invaded India in 1193 and set up his own dynasty. Muslim armies went further east and south. A Muslim general, Bakhtiyar Khilji, went through Bihar and destroyed all vestiges of Buddhism in that region.

These earlier Muslim invaders were Turks. It was more the spirit of vandalism than the love of spreading Islam that fired their iconoclasm. They did great disservice to the memory of their Prophet and the gospel that he had preached. Muslims never succeeded in erasing the awesome image the Turks had created of Islam in the Hindu mind. Thereafter, the Hindu looked upon Islam as an alien religion, regarded the Muslims as ruthless barbarians and Indians who accepted Islam either through fear or favour as collaborators and outcasts.

The change in the Hindus' attitude towards the Muslims came a long time after the Muslim crescent gave way to the Muslim missionary. And even then not in a measure to bring about a real change of heart.

In the wake of Muslim conquerors came many Islamic scholars and divines who made their homes in India; the most remarkable of them were known as Sufis (those who were of wool, *suf*). These men were mystics who lived like hermits on the outskirts of cities. While the militant Muslims sought to spread Islam through conquest, the Sufis did so through understanding of the other faiths and demonstrating the superiority of Islam. Had not the holy Prophet said, "Whichever way ye turn, there is the face of Allah?" So the Sufis turned for inspiration in all directions. They studied neo-Platonic Greek philosophy, the mystic movements of the Jews, Christians and Buddhists. And despite the fact that the Prophet had said there should be "no monasticism in Islam", they set up monastic orders of their own.

The Sufis said that men should not only fear the wrath of God, but at the same time love Him and submit to His will. "Love of God hath so absorbed me that neither love nor hate of any other thing remains in my heart," wrote Rabia (AD 801), a Sufi poetess. Complete submission to the will of Allah was summed up in the litany that the Sufis chanted: *"Alaika tawakkultu*" ("Lord, in Thee have I trusted"). Sufis believed that the most effective way of gaining converts was by leading exemplary lives, by serving the common people and stringing their hearts on the rosary of love (*talif-i-kulub*).

In the fourth and fifth centuries of the *Hejira*, the Sufis developed many practices already known to Hindu mystic orders. The Sufi litany (*dhikr*) was not unlike the Hindu *mantra*. While the Hindu mystic went into samadhi to commune with God, the Sufi did it by intense meditation and passing into a trance (*sama*). The Hindus emphasised the need for a spiritual mentor, the guru, to direct the disciple (*chela*) along the right spiritual path. So did the Sufis. "The way of faith is obscure, but the Devil's ways are many and patent and he who has no Shaikh to guide him will be led by the Devil into his ways," wrote Al Ghazzali, a twelfth century Sufi divine. The Hindus had their *maths* and *ashrams*, the Sufis had their hospices (*khanqahs*) where they, like the Hindus, composed poetry (often erotic), with spiritual *double-entendre*, sang songs of praise of the Prophet (*naat-i-rasul*) and danced in ecstasy. The aim of the Sufi was the same as that of the Hindu mystic – to merge his identity with God and so become God. The Hindu mystic when he attained union with God exclaimed: "*Aham Brahma asmi*" – "I am God." In a similar state of mystic exaltation the Sufi would explode: "*Anal haq*" – "I am reality."

The Sufis who came to India belonged to different orders with slightly differing practices. Four orders deserve attention. In the order of importance they were: the Chistiya, the Suhrawardiya, the Qadiriya and the Naqshabandi. The first orders immediately proceeded to take Hindus in their embrace of friendship. It is they, chiefly the Chistiyas, who won many converts to Islam. In order to gain the confidence of the Hindus, the Sufis not only read Hindu religious texts and spoke reverently of Hindu gods but also fraternised with them. In their eagerness, they often "out Hindu'd the Hindu", wrote Sir Mohammed Iqbal. The tombs of the Chishti saints – notably of Khwaja Mueenuddin at Ajmer, Farid Shakarganj at Pak Pattan (now in Pakistan), Qutubuddin Bakhtiyar Kaki, Nizamuddin Auliya and Nasiruddin Roshan Chiragh in Delhi became places of pilgrimage for Indian Muslims.

The vast majority of Indian Muslims are converts from Hinduism and therefore of the same race as the Hindus. Most of the converts came from the lower castes and accepted Islam, not from fear of persecution or to earn favour with their masters, but because they were unhappy with the higher castes' discrimination against them and because they found the simplicity of Islamic do's and don'ts more to their liking than the tortuous metaphysics of Brahmanical Hinduism.

Indian Muslims represent various shades of Islamic fervour ranging from the absolute purists down to the very Hinduised. Like Muslims elsewhere in the world, Indian Muslims have two major divisions, the Sunnis, who form almost 70 per cent of their population and the Shias, who believe that Ali was the first caliph and the other three were usurpers. Shias are spread out all over India; their main centre is Lucknow. The hostility between the Shia and the Sunni is endemic. It often becomes violent during Muharram, when Shias mourn the martyrdom of the sons of Ali – Hassan and Hussain. Shias and Sunnis seldom intermarry. In private conversation they often refer to each other with abusive epithets, *khatmal* (bedbug) and *pissoo* (louse).

In Maharashtra and Gujarat there are many sub-sects of Muslims: Ismailis who include the Khoja followers of the Aga Khan, the Bohras – followers of the Syedna, and the Memons. Most of these Muslim communities observe many Hindu customs.

The points of conflict between Hinduism and Islam were too vital to allow the evolution of a faith which could combine the tenets of both. Islam was precise, monotheistic, authoritarian. Hinduism was vague, idolatrous and *laissez-faire*. Islam was egalitarian, at least it professed the fraternal equality of all Muslims. Hinduism was riven with castes. The Muslim way of life was also different. Muslims were polygamous, looked upon marriage as a contract which could be easily dissolved. They abstained from liquor but ate meat. They abhorred the hog but relished the cow. The Hindu (often polygamous himself) looked upon marriage as a sacrament and did not recognise divorce. He did not object to drink and if he was a meat-eater, he relished pork but was horrified at the very thought of hurting a cow which he looked upon as *go-mata*, the cow-mother. He regarded cow-killers as unclean (*mlechha*) abominations.

Among both the Hindus and the Muslims two distinct points of view emerged on the kind of relationship which could be established with each other.

Amongst Muslims, the ruling classes, frequently of non-Indian origin, believed that Hindus should be treated as second-class citizens. Since there were too many of them and too few willing to accept Islam, it followed that they should be ruled by an iron hand; if necessary, they were to be terrorised by pogroms, massacres and the destruction of their temples. They were also to be forced to pay *jiziya* – a tax imposed on infidels in lieu of exemption from military service.

When Muslims ceased to be politically dominant, India automatically ceased to be *Dar-ul-Islam* and became *Dar-ul-Harab* (sphere of war). Then Muslims were to look upon themselves as a nation apart from the Hindus. This point of view was generally accepted by the Muslims; hence few Muslims joined the Hindu-dominated freedom movement against the British. Moreover, there were hardly any Muslims in the terrorist organisations. These Muslims came to subscribe to the "two-nation" theory, viz., that they, the Muslims, had nothing in common with the Hindus and must strive towards creating a state of their own.

There was, however, another Muslim point of view expressed in the sentiment, "We are Indians first, Muslims afterwards. Although we must retain our religious identity we must collaborate with our Hindu countrymen." For a few years between 1917 and 1920 this point of view gained acceptance amongst the Muslim masses. Thereafter, the majority went over to the two-nation theory which resulted in the formation of Pakistan.

The Hindus also had two distinct attitudes towards the Muslims. Most Hindus continued to regard the Muslims as foreigners with extra-territorial loyalties. Muslims, they said, were emotionally more involved with their co-religionists in Turkey, Egypt, Palestine, Persia and Arabia than with their non-Muslim countrymen. Their enthusiasm for Pan-Islamic movements was cited as evidence. These Hindus also accepted the two-nation theory. The Bharatiya Janata Party (erstwhile Bharatiya Jan Sangh) and the RSS are the chief propagandists of this point of view today.

A smaller but enlightened minority of Hindu liberals were for assimilating the Muslims in India's social life. They were strongly backed by some religious leaders like Rammohan Roy, Ramakrishna Paramhamsa, Vivekananda. Sri Aurobindo, and above all, the politician-saint, Mahatma Gandhi. It was due to Gandhi's enormous influence that the policy of befriending the Muslims was accepted by the Hindu masses. Nehru gave this sentiment concrete shape by declaring India a secular state. Mrs Indira Gandhi continued to strive for the integration of over 75 million Muslims in the mainstream of Indianism.

7

Indian Christians

*C*hristians, numbering over 16.1 million or 2.43 per cent of the population, are, next to the Muslims, the second largest religious minority of India.

Christianity, like Islam, was introduced into India by foreigners. Although never in its history was it rammed down the throats of the unwilling heathen, much of its proselytisation was carried out under the patronage of Christian rulers and often induced by hopes of worldly gain. As a result, despite the enormous educational, medical and social work done by Christians they are looked upon with a kind of benign contempt (a common epithet used for them in Maharashtra is *makapaon* – bread-eater), and several states have passed legislation restricting Christian missionary activity.

Christianity came very early to India. Thomas Didymus, the apostle, came to Malabar in the year AD 52. Although his mission was to convert Jews who had preceded him to India, once in the country, he decided to take on the gentile heathen. For his pains, the gentiles murdered him. Nothing more was heard of Christianity in India for three centuries.

In the year AD 345 Thomas of Canaan, a merchant prince, brought 72 Christian families (about 400 men and women) from Syria. They became the nucleus of the Syrian Church in Malabar. After the Arabs became masters of the seas, there was little communication between the Syrian Christians of India and the Christians of the Middle East.

(Some European missionaries like Friar John of Monte Corvino did briefly appear on the scene in AD 1291-92 but made little impact.)

The Syrian Christian community of present-day Kerala is one of the oldest in Christendom. Many of their names derive from the Old Testament, e.g., Matthai (from Matthew), Verughese, and Thomas from their founder and patron-saint.

In AD 1498 Vasco da Gama landed at Calicut. At that time, it is estimated that the number of Syrian

Vasco da Gama

Christians had increased to 200,000. Portuguese seamen were welcomed by the Syrians as well as by the Hindus. The fraternisation was brief, because by now the Syrians had come to share the Hindus' abhorrence for beef and were somewhat put out by the high style of living of the Portuguese Fathers. The Portuguese were unable to mix with the natives and came to be known by the pejorative *parang* (foreigner).

The first important Catholic settlement began in 1510 when the Portuguese commander, Albuquerque, took Goa. He brought Franciscan and Dominican priests with him. The greatest figure amongst them was St Francis Xavier, who arrived in AD 1542 and preached the Gospel to the fisher folk, living along the west coast between Goa and Cape Comorin. After some years Francis Xavier went to

St Francis Xavier

Japan. On his way back to India he died at Canton in December AD 1552. His body was brought to Goa, where it was on view in a state of preservation, till it was interred a few years ago.

Goa remains to this day the main centre of Catholic Christianity in India. Most Goan Christians bear Portuguese names: De Mellow, De Souza, Pereira, Dias, De Silva, De Cunha, Noronha, etc. Their lighter skins also establish a certain amount of intermarriage with the Portuguese settlers. For many years under British rule, because of their familiarity with European cuisine and music, the Goans' chief occupation was to serve in restaurants as chefs, waiters or musicians. Since independence, they have branched out in different professions and today occupy high positions, as governors, ministers, generals and ambassadors. Quite a few have resumed Indian names.

The chief stumbling block in the way of the Christian missionary was the Hindu caste system. He found it easy enough to convert the untouchables – the higher castes could not care less, but he soon found that being Christian became synonymous with being an untouchable, an outcast. An ingenious attempt to proselytise the Brahmins was made by Robert de Nobili and Father Rico who described themselves as Brahmin Christians from Rome. They wore caste marks, learnt Sanskrit and Tamil and, like orthodox Brahmins, disdained contact with the lower castes. In ten years of preaching, de Nobili is said to have converted 100,000 Brahmins (a vast exaggeration). But de Nobili was censured by the Franciscans who worked amongst the untouchables and his mission was closed.

Till the sixteenth century Christianity remained confined to the South and was divided into two groups: the Syrians in Malabar and the Roman Catholics in Portuguese Goa.

Valiant efforts were made by the Jesuits to convert

the Mughal Emperor, Akbar (AD 1556-1605). A Jesuit mission responded to the Emperor's invitation and arrived at Agra in AD 1578. It was well received. But its spokesmen soon found themselves out of their depth in argument with Muslim and Hindu theologians. A second mission consisting of more erudite Catholics followed and spent over three years in pointless debate on points of theology with their Hindu and Muslim counterparts. By then, the Emperor had begun to take large doses of laudanum and was more inclined to drop off to sleep than listen to scholarly disputation about God, angels, heaven and hell. His majesty was courteous as ever but the closest he came to accepting Christianity was to add a Christian lady to his already well-stocked harem of Muslim, Hindu, Jewish and Armenian women.

The Jesuits' hope revived with the accession of Akbar's son, Jehangir (AD 1605-27). The new emperor also heard the Jesuits with respect and even allowed two of his nephews to be converted to Christianity. That was all. His respect for Christianity was somewhat diminished by the wranglings between the Portuguese Roman Catholics and the Protestant English Ambassadors, Captain Hawkins and Sir Thomas Roe. An incident illustrates the religious atmosphere that prevailed in Agra at the time. The Jesuits produced a very religious-minded monkey at court. The Emperor wrote down the names of twelve prophets on a set of twelve cards and held them out to the monkey. The monkey reverently picked up one bearing the name of Jesus. Muslim and Hindu courtiers protested that they had seen the monkey-owner make a signal to his pet. The names of the twelve prophets were rewritten in code unknown to the owner of the monkey and once more held out for selection. The ape once again picked up the card which bore the name of Jesus. The Muslims and Hindus created an uproar that this time also the master had signalled to his monkey. A third time the Emperor wrote the names of the prophets, omitting the name of Jesus, the monkey scrutinised the cards and when it could not spot the holy name of Jesus, it went into a rage and tore up the cards. Sir Thomas Roe, who was present at the performance, noted in his report that this was a "trick of the Jesuits".

In 1627 the Emperor Jehangir died. With him died hopes of Christianising India by converting its ruler. As a matter of fact, no ruler of any princely state ever accepted the Christian faith. A doubtful exception was the colourful Begum Zebunnissa Joanna Samru (AD 1836) of Sardana, near Delhi, who also acquired a succession of European lovers before she married a German Catholic, Walter Reinhardt. The Papacy conferred the title of Joanna Nobilis on her.

Protestant Missions

Three Protestant powers which occupied different parts of Indian territory were the Dutch, the Danes and the English (who were more interested in profit than in proselytising and had a strong anti-missionary bias). The Dutch were more religious-minded. They set up a mission in AD 1706; in AD 1711 the first Protestant church was built on Dutch property.

Protestant missionaries had to encounter the same difficulties as the Catholics. The Indians tended to judge the professions of the missionaries by the practice of the white communities. The way of life of the white settler did not arouse the admiration of the natives. Terry, an Englishman, records the reaction of an outspoken Indian: "Christian religion, devil religion; Christians much drink."

Schwartz (AD 1798), another notable evangelist, records that once when he was taking the Indian air, he met a Hindu friend in the company of a prostitute. He was shocked and admonished the Hindu that if he continued to keep the company of ladies of ill repute he would not go to the Kingdom of Heaven. "In that case," cut in the lady tartly, "hardly any European will enter it."

Protestantism made its real impact on India in the last years of the eighteenth century through the labours of the Baptists. William Carey arrived in Calcutta in AD 1793 and, finding the British officials hostile, set up his mission in Danish territory at Serampur. Although Carey gained no converts in his first seven years at Serampur, he organised the translation of the Bible in 36 languages and put up a printing press to publish them. Serampur became a centre of Christian knowledge. It was raised to the status of a college and then to a university.

British officials' attitude towards proselytisation changed. They turned a blind eye to the Governor-General's undertaking "to preserve the laws of the *Shastras* and the Quran and to protect the natives of India in the free exercise of their religion," and inserted a clause in the charter which allowed missionaries "to instruct the gentile".

The freedom "to instruct the gentoos" which came to be known as "the pious clause" was given legal sanction and English missionaries started entering India in larger numbers. The anti-missionary clique, however, remained strong and ascribed the resentment of the Indians towards the English to the attacks of the missionaries' on Hinduism and Islam.

The first American Protestant missionaries arrived at Calcutta in 1812. Twenty years later American Presbyterians opened a centre in 1834 at Ludhiana in the Punjab. Thereafter, there was a constant flow of American missionaries to different parts of India. The Baptists concentrated their energies on the tribal belt extending from the Assam hills down to Central India. The Presbyterians were mainly in the rural areas of northern India. By 1910 there were 1,800 American missionaries in the country. The Americans profited from the experiences of their European predecessors. They lived modestly and being of puritan stock did not indulge in drink. Besides, there were no American civilians or soldiers in India to give them a bad name. They did splendid work opening schools and colleges, hospitals, lepresariums, community centres, introducing new methods of farming, fruit cultivation and cattle-breeding. Many American names came to be mentioned with respect and gratitude: Lowrig, Reed, Lucas, Ewing, Wannamaker. The following institutions are amongst the more famous: The Ludhiana Hospital under Drs Newton and James Campbell; the Gordon Christian College (named after Rev Andrew Gordon) at Rawalpindi; the Baring Christian College at Gurdaspur; the Forman Christian College and Ewing Hostel at Lahore; the Bethune College (1849) at Calcutta; the Isabella Thoburn and Reid Christian College at Lucknow.

American missionaries compiled and published the earliest grammars and dictionaries of Pubjabi, Hindi, Urdu and Marathi. They issued journals: The *Nur Afshan* (The Light), an Urdu weekly from Ludhiana; *Orunoday* (Rising Sun) in Assamese; *Gyanoday* (Light of Knowledge) in Marathi.

Christian missions, Catholic as well as Protestant, European as well as American, also did commendable work during famines. Although the Hindus sneered at the "rice converts" they made during these years of distress, they at least filled the bowls of the hungry with food – which was more than was done by any religious organisations of the Hindus or Muslims. In the 1891 famine, the Methodists gained 15,000 converts. Another neglected people, the tribes who lived by crime (and are listed in the Criminal Tribes Act of 1871), were ministered to by the Salvation Army.

Evangelism was of secondary interest to the Protestant missionary. Nevertheless, mass conversions followed good works. In 1851 there were 90,000 Protestant Christians; by 1871 the numbers had more than doubled. By 1921 the Protestants constituted 1.5 per cent of the population of India, more than a half of whom owed their Christianisation to American missionary zeal.

More far-reaching than the number of converts it made was the influence of Protestantism on Hinduism. Protesants took active part in the suppression of *sati* (outlawed in 1829), ending female infanticide, and suppressing the Thugs; alleviating the condition of Hindu widows and temple prostitutes; raising the age of marriage, etc. It was the Christian missionaries' *nishkama karma* which roused the admiration of Hindu reformers like Rammohan Roy, whose *Brahmo Samaj,* set up in 1828 drew a great deal of its inspiration from Christianity. So also did the *Prarthana Samaj* (set up in 1867) in Maharashtra and Gujarat. It soon became a two-way traffic of ideas. Emerson, Thoreau and Walt Whitman acknowledged their debt to Vedanta in their writings. The association of a large number of white Christians with the Indian freedom movement, starting with Allan Octavian Hume, the first President of the Indian National Congress, down to the associates of Mahatma Gandhi (C.F. Andrews, Stanley

Jones, Fred B. Fisher, Clifford Manshardt, Stokes) went a long way towards changing the popular misconception that Christianity was only the other side of the Imperialist coin.

Nevertheless, Christianity did not make as strong an impact on India as one might have expected, considering the pressure of political power, the money spent and the enlightened, dedicated social work put in by thousands of missionaries. The chief reason for this was that Christianity was never able to erase the taint of being alien to the soil of India. Efforts made to Indianise Christianity had a limited success. Many Christians continued to bear high-sounding English names, their women wore a comical mixture of European and Indian dress; their hymns translated into Indian languages and sung to outlandish tunes to the accompaniment of harmoniums, cymbals and drums, evoked more derision than reverence.

India did not produce a Christian saint of its own. And saints have great importance in Indian eyes. Only one, Sadhu Sunder Singh, a Sikh convert, came close to wearing a halo. Other leaders thrown up by the Indian Christian community were good men but without the charisma of sainthood. Such were Azariah, K.T. Paul, J.R. Chitambar, S.K. Rudra and S.N. Mukerjee; women like Pandita Ramabai of Maharashtra, Mrs Chatterjee of Delhi and Miss Sarkur of the Punjab were hardly known outside Christian circles. What Christianity needed in the Indian setting was a

Mahatma; all it produced were men and women, good scouts, girl guides, directors and YMCA and YWCA.

Hinduism has taken Christianity in its stride. It has greater appeal for the sophisticated Indian mind than the simple tenets of Christianity. And the Indian, much as he admires good works, is loathe to put himself out or give credit to those who do them. To him a Christian is not really 100 per cent Indian. Not a Hindu voice was raised in protest against the Government's Hindu-oriented discrimination (wrongly described as the Freedom of Religion Act) against Christian missionaries, many of whom were expelled from the country on unproven charges of being foreign agents.

8

The Sikhs

Sikhs form over 2 per cent of the population of India. In the reckoning of heads they are, after the Muslims and Christians, the third on the list of minorities. But certain factors give the Sikhs an importance far beyond their numbers. First, unlike the Muslims and the Christians who are scattered all over the country, the Sikhs are concentrated in one area: over 80 per cent of them are in East Punjab where they now form a majority. Secondly, they are on the most sensitive frontier of India – the one separating India from Pakistan. A large proportion of the land forces of both the nations face each other on this border. It was the scene of hostilities in the autumn of 1965 and in December 1971 and will inevitably be the arena of future confrontation between India and Pakistan.

Thirdly, all Sikhs speak one language, Punjabi; other minorities, being scattered, speak languages of the region they inhabit and do not therefore have the linguistic unity which binds the Sikhs. Fourthly, the Sikhs have a very important role in the defence services of India. At one time under British rule, almost 30 per cent of the British Indian army was Sikh; even today, between 15 and 20 per cent of India's defence personnel are Sikhs. Fifthly, the Sikhs are more politically conscious than other Indians. The Shiromani Gurdwara Prabandhak Committee (SGPC), meant to administer the Sikh historical shrines, is an elected body; it controls large funds and consequently wields enormous patronage in the appointment of caretakers of temples and staff for the innumerable schools, colleges, hospitals and orphanages it has to administer. The SGPC is a sort of Sikh Parliament in whose proceedings they take as much interest as they do in the proceedings of the state and central legislatures. Sixthly, the Sikhs, next to the Parsis, are the most prosperous community of India. Although their fortunes suffered a crippling loss in 1947, when they had to abandon their richest lands to Pakistan, they quickly rehabilitated themselves in India and regained much of their lost prosperity. In a country infested with beggars, it is rare to see a Sikh stretch out his hand for alms. They are India's most progressive farmers and small-scale entrepreneurs, and virtually control the road transport systems of many states of northern

India. Their standards of literacy as well as of living are higher than those prevailing in other communities. They are the best fed, the ablest-bodied and the longest-living people of the country. They dominate the field of sports, forming almost a half of India's contingent to any Olympic contest. Of the nine Indians that scaled the Everest in 1965, three atop the peak and the leader of the team, were Sikhs.

All these factors have gone to make the Sikh outgoing, assertive and aggressive. No one can say that his faith, like that of the Muslims and the Christians, was brought from other lands. Nor can anyone accuse him of extra-territorial loyalties. In the four centuries of his existence he has developed a kind of one-upmanship expressed in the song, "Anything you can do, I can do better." He looks upon himself as one of a chosen people. He refers to himself as *sava lakh* – equal to a hundred and twenty-five thousand others or a *fauj* (an army). The Sikh is the butt of humour. The "Sardarji joke" is based on a stereotype which makes him out to be naïve, slow-witted and, at noontime, dangerously mad.

Let us now see what has made the Sikh what he is today.

★

The word Sikh is derived from the Sanskrit *shishya* or the Pali *sikkha*, meaning disciple. The Sikhs are the disciples of their ten gurus and worship a book, the

Granth Sahib, which is a compilation of hymns composed by the gurus and other saints of India, both Hindus and Muslims. The Sikh Gurdwaras Act defines a Sikh as "one who believes in the ten gurus and the *Granth Sahib*".

Granth Sahib (EK OM KAR)
Khanda Sahib

Nanak, the first guru of the Sikhs, was born in AD 1469 in a village about forty miles from Lahore (now in Pakistan). His parents were Hindus belonging to a Kshatriya sub-sect known as Bedis, i.e., those who know the Vedas. Nanak was taught a little Arabic, Persian, some Sanskrit, Hindi and accounting. But his mind was never in his work. He spent his time meditating and seeking the company of wandering hermits. His parents found a wife for him. They had two sons. Nanak soon lost interest in his family and once again reverted to meditating and wandering. His elder sister took him away with her and for a time he worked as an accountant in the office of the local Muslim chieftain. The urge to abandon worldly pursuits became too strong. A Muslim servant and rebeck-player, Mardana, joined him. Nanak began to compose hymns, Mardana set them to music and the two began to organise community hymn-singing.

In the year 1499, when Nanak was thirty years old he had a mystic experience. One morning while bathing in a stream he disappeared under the water. According to his biographers, he found himself in the presence of God who spoke to him thus:

"Nanak, I am with thee. Through thee will my Name be magnified. Go into the world to pray and teach mankind how to pray. But be not sullied by the ways of the world. Let thine life be one of praise of the Word (*Nam*), of charity (*dan*), ablution (*ishnan*), service (*seva*) and prayer (*simran*)."

Nanak was missing for three days and nights. When he came back, the first thing he said to the people who thronged to greet him was, "There is no Hindu; there is no Mussalman."

Nanak took to preaching. He and his first disciple, the Muslim Mardana, travelled extensively in India and abroad. We are not certain of these travels but according to Sikh tradition, the guru undertook four long voyages – eastwards as far as Assam, southwards down to Sri Lanka, westwards to Mecca and beyond, and finally, to the hills and plains of the Punjab. He visited many holy cities of the

Guru Nanak

Hindus and the Muslims, pointing out the folly of meaningless ritual and emphasising the common aspects of the two faiths. He spent his last years in a town called Kartarpur, meaning "The-abode-of-the-Creator" – preaching, composing, and singing hymns. He died in 1539 at the age of seventy. He was acclaimed by both the Hindus and the Muslims as the king of holy men.

Nanak's teaching reveals the influence of Hinduism and Islam. By the fifteenth century these religious systems had evolved some beliefs which had much in common. It was from the teachings of the Muslim Sufis – notably Sheikh Farid and the *Bhaktas* (primarily Kabir) – that Nanak drew his inspiration. From Islam Nanak took its unqualified monotheism, rejection of idolatry and the caste system. From Hinduism he borrowed the metaphysics of the Upanishads and the Gita. He elevated reality (*sat*) to the position of the One Supreme God. He accepted the theory of *karma* and transmigration of souls. The path he advocated was to *Bhakti* emphasising the worship of the name of God (*Nam-marga*). He rejected asceticism and propagated the *grihastha-dharma* (religion for the house holder) and advocated the necessity of taking on a guru and keeping company with holy men (*sadh sangat*).

Nanak set great store by community hymn-singing (*kirtan*). He advised his followers to rise before dawn and listen to religious music, for he believed that in the stillness of the ambrosial hours (*amritvela*), one is best able to commune with God.

When Nanak died he left behind him a small community of Hindus and Muslims who described themselves as *Nanak-panthis* – followers of Nanak's way. He appointed one of his disciples, Angad, to be the second guru. Angad, when dying, appointed one of his disciples as the third guru. By then the community of Sikhs had increased and many places of worship (dharamsalas or gurdwaras) had to be maintained from offerings made by followers. As often happens in the Orient, when property is involved, succession, even to a spiritual institution, follows the laws of inheritance. The succeeding seven gurus were members of one family.

It was with the fifth guru, Arjun, that Sikhism was established as a separate religious system. Arjun was Sikhism's St Paul, the builder of the Sikh Church. He put together the writings of his predecessors, his own compositions (he was an uncommonly good poet) and those of Hindu and Muslim saints and gave the Sikhs a holy book of their own – the *Adi Granth*. He made

Golden Temple

Amritsar into an important trade centre and raised a temple which became a place of pilgrimage. He became a rich merchant-prince with a large following. The Mughal government as well as the leading Hindus who saw the masses turning from Hinduism to Sikhism were perturbed by his success. Arjun was arrested and tortured in jail where he died (1606). He became the first martyr of the Sikhs.

Arjun's son, Hargobind, who succeeded him, took up arms. He too was gaoled by the Mughal authorities. The same fate befell the ninth guru, Tegh Bahadur, who was beheaded at Delhi in the year 1675. Tegh Bahadur's son, Gobind, finally transformed the pacificist Sikhs into a militant fraternity he named the Khalsa (from the Persian *Khalis*, meaning "the pure"). He announced the change in a dramatic way on the Hindu New Year's Day in the spring of the year 1699. Before an assembly of over 80,000 Sikhs he asked for the heads of five for sacrifice. One by one he took these five behind a tent and came out with his sword dripping with blood. (He slew five goats instead.) These five were the first batch of Khalsa. Thereafter, several thousand were baptised by drinking sweetened water, *amrit* (nectar), from a common bowl. They swore to observe five vows: to wear their hair and beards unshorn (*kesh*) and carry a comb (*kangha*) to keep them tidy; to wear the soldier's breeches (*kucch*); to wear a steel bracelet on their right wrist (*kada*); and to carry a sabre (*kirpan*) on their person.

Since baptism was a new birth, the baptised were given new names. All males were to bear the name "Singh", common amongst Indian martial tribes, so that their caste names may be obliterated.(Similarly Sikh women were to use the surname "Kaur".) The guru explained these changes:

"I wish you all to embrace one creed and follow one path, obliterating all differences of religion. Let the four Hindu castes, who have different rules laid down for them in the *Shastras*, abandon them altogether and, adopting the way of cooperation, mix freely with one another. Let no one deem himself superior to another. Let no one pay heed to the Ganges and other places of pilgrimage considered holy in the Hindu religion or adore the Hindu deities."

Not all Sikhs accepted the Guru's innovations. Those who preferred to follow only the earlier gurus came to be known as *Sahajdharis* (slow-adopters). Only Gobind's followers became the hirsute, beturbaned Khalsa.

Guru Gobind spent the remaining eight years of his life fighting the neighbouring Hindu rajas and the Mughals. He lost all his four sons – two were killed fighting; two younger boys were captured and executed. And finally he himself was assassinated by Mughal hirelings.

Before his death, he declared the succession of gurus at an end and exhorted the Sikhs to look upon the *Adi Granth*, compiled by the fifth guru, as the symbolic representation of all the ten gurus.

Four years after the death of Gobind, the Sikhs rose under Banda, a leader appointed by the guru, and virtually destroyed the Mughal administration in the Punjab. Banda was eventually captured and executed. But thereafter, there was no holding back the Sikhs. They formed themselves into bands of guerilla fighters (*misls*) and harassed the Mughals. They were helped by fresh invasions of Persians and Afghans from the north-west. While the Mughals faced the invaders in the open and suffered many defeats, Sikh guerilla bands discreetly retreated into the jungles and mountains, only to re-emerge to prey upon the loot-laden caravans of the conquerors. They had more than their share of reverses. But with the peasantry behind them, their numbers increased and they grew from strength to strength. By the middle of the eighteenth century, Sikh *misls* controlled the whole of northern India from the Indus to the Ganges and levelled a tax, *Raakhi* (Protection money), on the landowners.

Out of these *misls*, the Sukarchakias emerged stronger than the others. It was the scion of this *misl*, the one-eyed Ranjit Singh who, for a brief period of forty years, became Maharajah of the Punjab. He defeated the Afghans, the Patinas and the Kashmiris. His kingdom extended from Afghanistan to the mountain ranges dividing India and China, along the Sutlej and down to the borders of Sindh.

Ranjit Singh died in 1839. Within ten years the kingdom of the Sikhs collapsed. In a succession of bloody battles fought between 1845 and 1849, the British emerged victors and annexed the Sikhs' domains to their empire.

The British were sagacious enough to recognise the fighting qualities of the Sikhs and offered them service in the Company's forces. The Sikhs became the favoured mercenaries of the British. They fought on the British side against the mutineers in 1857; they policed the British Empire from Shanghai, the Malaya States, Burma, and Singapore to the Persian Gulf. They were rewarded with lands and given preferential treatment in the services. All this continued right up to World War I.

Two aspects of the development of Sikhism should be borne in mind. First, Sikhism, which had started as a kind of bridge between the Hindus and the Muslims, soon became the spearhead against Mughal-Muslim tyranny. Most of the converts to Sikhism were, therefore, Hindus who brought with them their religious and social practices. Muslims began to look upon the Sikhs as simply aggressive, bearded Hindus. ("A kind of vicious Hindu," Dr Lorimer once described them.)

Second, since the overwhelming majority of converts to Sikhism were Hindus and Hindus were more than eager to intermarry with them, the Sikhs were faced with the problem of maintaining their separate identity. The growing of long hair and beards became *de rigeur*, the *Sahajdharis* came to be looked upon as second-class Sikhs, only a little better than renegades (*patit*). Practices which distinguished them from the Hindus gained exaggerated emphasis. Thus smoking was strictly forbidden; drinking often forgiven, even condoned. The British helped the Sikhs in this struggle for a separate identity by making the observance of Khalsa traditions compulsory for Sikh soldiers and civil servants. They gave Sikhs a separate electorate and reserved seats for them in legislative bodies.

With independence went the special privileges enjoyed by the Sikhs. So also the economic motives to conform to the Khalsa tradition of growing their hair and beards unshorn. Large numbers of young Sikhs began to abandon the Khalsa tradition and chose the easier path of the *Sahajdharis*. The dividing line between Hinduism and Sikhism being so thin, that the Sikhs were faced with the danger of extinction by relapsing back into the Hindu fold. The problem of identity is the most important that the Sikhs of today have to face.

9

The Parsis

*T*he number of Parsis is now less than 100,000, most of them living in the city of Bombay. It is a dying community; the rate of death is higher than the rate of birth; they admit no converts nor recognise offspring of non-Parsi fathers as Parsis. An increasing number of Parsi girls now marry outside the community.

The Parsis have made their mark on the industrial and social life of the country. They are the richest community of India and the only one with 100 per cent literacy. They control many industries, which they run on modern lines. The best known are the house of Tatas with interests in steel, automobiles, airlines, textiles, etc. and Godrej: safes, air-conditioners, steel furniture, etc. Parsi charities account for many schools, colleges, hospitals and picture galleries in Bombay.

Parsis are Zoroastrians by faith, Iranian-Aryans by race. (The word "Parsi" is derived from Farsi, meaning "Persian".) They fled from Iran at different periods of Muslim persecution of non-Muslims. By the seventeenth century there was a sizeable Parsi community on the Gujarat coast. Hindu rulers gave them protection and freedom to worship their gods. In return, the Parsis adopted many Hindu customs and names (Patel, Desai, Gandhi, Mehta) and accepted Gujarati as their language. When the British came, the Parsis emigrated from rural Gujarat to Bombay and readily Europeanised themselves. Many of their names, e.g. Contractor, Engineer, Carpenter, Readymoney, etc., bear testimony to their eagerness to be more easily understood by the English. Despite the fact that some Parsis took a prominent part in the Indian freedom movement (Dadabhai Naoroji, Shapur Saklatvala, Jhabvala, Nariman), the Indians have not forgiven them for favouring the British and their continuing enthusiasm for Iran. Many Parsis prefer to describe themselves as Iranians (Persians) rather than Indians.

Zoroastrian

Zoroastrianism is one of the world's oldest religions. The founder Zoroaster, or Zarathustra, is said to have lived at least 300 years before Alexander. Some scholars put his birth as far back as 1000 BC.

Zarathustra belonged to the Spitama clan and was the third of the five sons born to a pious scholar, Pourushaspa, and his wife, Dughdova. At the age of fifteen he left home and spent several years wandering and meditating. It was during his wanderings that he had a vision of God. He spent the rest of his life preaching. He was persecuted and when persecution failed to silence him, he was put in gaol. He was killed at the age of seventy-seven while defending his temple.

Zoroaster did not profess to teach a new religion but to restore the ancient *Mazda-yasni* – the belief in One, Omniscient God, Mazda. Zoroaster was an *avatar*, in ancient Persian a *saoshyant*, sent to cleanse people of evil and stop them worshipping devils (*daeva-yasni*).

According to Zoroastrian belief, Ahura Mazda is the good and all-wise God and Angra Mainyu, the evil spirit. Zoroaster's hymns, called the *Gathas*, form the oldest part of the scripture, the *Zend-Avesta*.

Although Ahura Mazda is the only one and the supreme deity, Zoroaster permitted the worship of six other "divine intelligences" as attributes of Ahura Mazda. These are: the good mind (*vohu manah*); the best order (*asha vahishta*); absolute power (*kshathra vairya*); high thought (*armaiti*); perfection (*haurvatat*); and immortality (*ameretat*).

Zoroaster regarded fire as a *symbolic* representation of the son of Ahura Mazda (*puthro shuraha Mazdao*). In all Zoroastrian temples, known as *atash behrams* or *agiaris*, a sacred flame is constantly kept burning. Zoroaster also considered water and earth pure and forbade their pollution.

Zoroaster emphasised the necessity for work. "What is the way for furthering the *Mazda-Yasnan* religion?" someone asked God. He replied, "Unceasing cultivation of corn. Whosoever cultivates corn, cultivates righteousness…"

Zoroastrians do not believe in asceticism. Their faith is summed up in the litany which they recite thrice every morning *Vispa humata, vispa hukhta, vispa avarshta* – a man's good thoughts, good words and good deeds lead him to heaven; his bad thoughts and bad words lead him to hell.

Parsi religious customs have taken much from the Hindus. At the age of seven a Parsi child has the *navjot*, when he or she is invested with a sacred shirt (*sudrah*) and the sacred thread (*kusti*). A Parsi marriage is, however, a contract and not a sacrament. Parsis have always been monogamous and permit divorce. Since Zoroaster declared fire, water and earth to be sacred, the Parsis dispose of their dead by exposing them to the sun in specially erected "Towers of Silence", where vultures pick them clean. In towns where there are no towers of silence, the Parsis bury their dead.

10

The Hindu Period

*T*ext-book writers divide the history of India into four periods: Hindu, Muslim, British and post-independence. There are, however, no precise beginnings or endings of these four periods, nor any historical justification for labelling them as Hindu, Muslim or British. The only justification is convenience – and now tradition. We too will sacrifice accuracy on the altar of convenience and tradition.

Archaeologists date human habitation in India to as far back as 400,000 BC. The evidence of slow and painful evolution of man from his simian ancestors can be seen on disinterred skulls, bones, implements of hunting, and tilling on display in many museums. This is prehistory or history of which we know no more than what sharpened flint or polished bone can tell.

The discovery of India's earliest civilisation is itself a story. Sometime in the middle of the nineteenth century, British engineers, engaged in linking the seaport of Karachi with the cities of the Punjab, needed stones and bricks to build solid foundations for the rail-track they were laying over the hundreds of miles of desert. The contract for supplying bricks was taken by two brothers who belonged to the region and who knew of an enormous hoard of sunbaked bricks buried under the sand. Instead of firing kilns, they dug up the required quantities of bricks and made an enormous profit. It was later discovered that these bricks had been baked at least 4,000 years ago.

In the 1920s the archaeological department of the Government of India decided to look into this story. As a result, two buried cities were excavated – Mohenjodaro ("mound of the dead"), along the Indus, and Harappa, some 400 miles north on the Ravi. Thereafter, many other excavations in the Punjab (notably Rupar) and Lothal in Gujarat yielded a bumper harvest of seals and terracotta, unfolding a tale of many cities that flourished sometime before 3000 BC. They were in a broad belt about 500 miles on each side of the river Indus and 1,000 miles along its course. Some cities, like Mohenjodaro, must have existed for many centuries as nine layers of buildings, one on top of the other were unearthed. Since these towns

Mohenjodaro

flourished about the same time and along an identifiable geographical belt and were linked by trade, the period in which they existed came to be known as the period of the Indus Valley Civilisation. It was contemporary with the Mesopotamian and the Nilotic civilisations.

A great deal has been written about the Indus Valley Civilisation. It is based on earthenware and pottery; metal jewellery, garments of wool and cotton; figurines of kings, warriors, dancing girls, trees, animals (real and imaginary), gods and goddesses and toys, which were excavated and are now housed in museums in Pakistan and India. The excavations prove the existence of wide roads, criss-crossing at right angles, waterways and sewage systems, public baths and meeting places. Funerary mounds, some with skeletons heaped together, indicate sudden death by violence or natural catastrophe which brought about the downfall of these cities.

Amongst the relics found were seals with pictographs which have not yet* yielded all their secrets. If and when the words are deciphered we may have a major breakthrough into India's past history. Till then, we accept what scholars like Mortimer Wheeler and Basham tell us about the Indus Valley civilisation, viz., that its halcyon years were between 3000 and 1500 BC, that the people who created this high level of urbanity can, for no better alternative, be described as Dravidians**, and that they were overcome by the ruffian-like Aryans mounted on swift-footed horses and driving chariots. These Aryans were Caucasians belonging to pastoral tribes living in villages (*grama*) under an elected chieftain (*raja*) who was advised by a council of elders (*sabha*), and, on cases touching the interests of the entire village, by the *samiti* (meeting of the village).

The Aryans brought with them a new language, Sanskrit. They developed this language in India. The Vedas, Upanishads and the Gita are examples of their

---

* Early in 1969 some scandinavian and later Indian scholars claimed to have deciphered the writing on the seals.

** Different racial types, ranging from the latin Mediterranean to the Polnesian Austroloid, are depicted amongst the human figures. The formation of skulls reveals the same ethnic diversity.

religious writing. Aryan writers achieved an equally high standard in drama and poetry.

By about 800 BC the Aryans learnt how to smelt iron ore and make ploughshares, utensils, swords and spears. Armed with these weapons they were able to forge ahead further east and southwards into India. It is likely that the eastward shift was due to the discovery of large deposits of iron ore in Bihar and the ability to sail boats in rivers and along the sea coast.

Centres of Aryan power shifted from the Punjab eastwards to Uttar Pradesh, Bihar and Orissa. New cities rose to prominence: Indraprastha (present-day Delhi), Hastinapur, Ayodhya, Kashi (Benares) and Pataliputra (Patna). This eastward shift had two consequences. Brahmanical Hinduism that the Aryans propagated was challenged by protest movements like Jainism and Buddhism, both of which originated in the eastern regions. At the same time, in their enthusiasm to push east and south, the Aryans neglected the defence of their rear and exposed the north-west to further invasions.

The Persians

The first to take advantage of the weakened frontier were the Persians under Cyrus, followed by Darius I (521-485 BC). Darius overran the Indus Valley. He recruited Punjabi soldiers in his army. Darius's son Xerxes used Punjabi foot soldiers when he invaded Greece (479 BC).

Although this Persian invasion was a passing phenomenon, it left a permanent impression on religion, art and administration. The solar cult of the Hindus is a Persian import. So also was the use of pillars to popularise laws. The investment of the chief with divinity to strengthen his position in society was taken by the Aryan chieftains from the Persians.

The next foreign intruders were the Greeks. Alexander of Macedonia overthrew Darius III in 331 BC and in the winter of 328-327 BC advanced into India. He was welcomed at Taxila and sumptuously entertained. Several thousand fatted calves were slaughtered to feed the invading hosts. Alexander proceeded inland to the Beas, and defeated King Porus and his vast army which included hundreds of war-elephants.

Kashipur Temple, Benares

Alexander was not able to penetrate much farther into the Punjab. He went down along the Indus to return home to die. Alexander's invasion was also a passing phenomenon. But he left behind him scattered colonies of Greeks who moulded the Indian style of art, architecture and sculpture.

Greek scribes noted the existence of marriage markets where poor parents sold their daughters and the practice of the immolation of widows on the funeral pyres of their dead husbands (*sati*).

The Mauryas

Indians did not take very long to react to the Greek invasion. A powerful Aryan dynasty, the Mauryas of Magadha (present-day Bihar), rose under Chandragupta (a popular name amongst Indian monarchs). He defeated the Greek general, Seleukus Nikator, in 305 BC and expanded his domains across the Indo-Gangetic plain from Bengal in the east to the heart of Afghanistan in the north-west. An account of his rule has been left by Megasthenes, Nikator's ambassador in the Mauryan court.

Megasthenes' original work has been lost. But Pliny quotes his eulogy to Indian civilisation: no slavery, peaceful husbandry, industry and chivalry of the men, virtuous chastity of women. He mentions the existence of several classes of Indian society – scholars, tillers, graziers and hunters, artisans and traders, police (including spies) and bureaucrats.

Chandragupta's twenty-four year reign is notable for a treatise on the art of government, *Arthashastra*, written by his minister, Kautilya (321-296 BC). Although Kautilya's thesis out-Machiavellies Machiavellianism both in age and in diabolic amorality, there is much more in it than the art of overcoming enemies and acquiring power. He gave advice on how a ruler could acquire and control a harem, on kinds of marital unions ("Marriage is the source of all disputes," wrote Kautilya) and other related topics. Kautilya suggested ways of employing spies and methods of administering poison to one's enemies. He is, however, best known for his thesis on the science of government. He made punishment (*dandaniti*) the basis of administration. His views on relations with neighbouring states are direct, pragmatic and full of common sense. He uses concentric circles (*mandalas*) to illustrate his point. Your neighbours are your natural enemies. Your neighbour's neighbours on the other side are his enemies and, therefore, your natural allies. In international affairs, more than in any others, said he, the law that operates is the *matsyanyaya* – the big fish eat the small. And so on.

Chandragupta Maurya was a Jain and like good Jains, ended his life by fasting to death.

Chandragupta's son, Bindusar (298-232 BC) added the Deccan to his domains. He exchanged envoys with the rulers of Egypt and Syria. And Bindusar's son, Asoka (273-232 BC), extended his sway further south into Mysore. Then he went to war to extend his territory across Orissa up to the Bay of Bengal. A bloody battle was fought at Kalinga (261 BC), giving a pyrrhic victory to Asoka. It is recorded that over 100,000 men were killed on the field of Kalinga. Asoka was so overcome with remorse that he renounced violence as an instrument of policy and turned to Buddhism for solace. He had his message of peace inscribed on rocks and pillars all over his domain. He preached non-violence and forbade the slaughter of animals for sacrifice. He sent out missionaries to propagate Buddhism. His son, Mahendra, became a monk and took the gospel of Buddha to Sri Lanka.

Asoka's is the greatest name in Indian history. His memory is perpetuated through the adaptation of one of his lion-based pillars (the lion representing the Buddha; Taurus the bull, the sign of his birth; and the wheel of law) as the official emblem of the Government of India today.

Maurya power petered out a hundred years after Asoka. New invasions of Bactrian Greeks dealt the *coup de grace*. During these centuries of breakup, the Brahmin Sungas and Kanvas established themselves in the

Ashoka Chakra

Indo-Gangetic plain, while the Deccan came to be ruled by the Telugus. Though "the Lords of the Deccan" were Hindus, it was during their rule that Buddhist monks bored caves at Karle and raised stupas at Sanchi and Amaravati.

The South was divided into three kingdoms: The Cholas around present-day Madras; the Cheras in Kerala; and the Pandyas based in Madurai right down to Kanyakumari. Madurai became the centre of Tamil learning. Sometime within two or three centuries after the birth of Christ, great Tamil classics, anthologies, and the works of Kural were produced.

These powerful southern dynasties made their influence felt all around. The Tamils invaded Sri Lanka, traded with the Romans on one side (gold Roman coins have been found in Tamil Nadu) and the countries of the Far East on the other. With sandalwood and spices, teak, ebony and ivory, the Tamilians exported Hinduism, Buddhism, Jainism, Indian philosophy, art and medicine.

While these changes were taking place, the Greeks again appeared in the north. Menander occupied the Punjab, made Sialkot his capital and then pushed eastwards. He invested the Mauryan capital Pataliputra (Patna) in 150 BC Greeks, known as *yavanas* (Ionians), accepted Indian religions. Menander himself accepted conversion to Buddhism. *The Questions of Milinda* (Menander) are a dialogue between the King and his Buddhist preceptor.

INDIA

Asoka's empire
(250 BC)

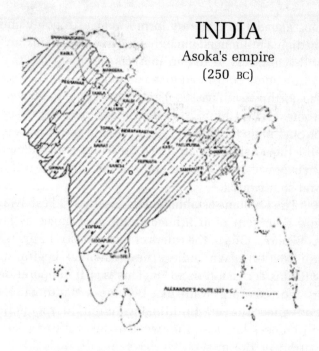

Although the Greeks readily Indianised themselves, they injected Greek blood into the culture of India. They taught Indians Greek methods of minting coins; Indian sculpture and painting became Greek-oriented. The centre of Greek culture was probably at Kandahar in Afghanistan; hence the style of sculpture and architecture came to be known as Gandhara. Hindu gods and goddesses assumed athletic Grecian forms and were wrapped in Hellenic drapery. The Greeks also popularised the dialogue (used earlier in the

Upanishads) as a literary form. Greek astronomy and medicine influenced the Indians. They opened up land and sea routes to Indian markets.

Invaders continued to make their inroads through the northwestern passes. This time, most of them were from western China. After the Greeks came the Sakas, or Scythians (*circa* 130 BC); after them the Parthians, and the Kushans. The first two tribes consolidated their power in the north and then pushed eastwards and southwards.

The Kushans established themselves at Peshawar and then sent their armies along the Ganges as far as Benares. One of the rulers of this dynasty, Kanishka (AD 78-144), gave India a new calendar beginning with his accession in AD 78. This is still in operation as the Saka era. Kanishka became a Buddhist. He convened the 4th Buddhist Council to reconcile differences between the two schisms. He was also a patron of the arts.

There is a hundred-year hiatus between the disintegration of the Kushans (AD 200) and the rise of the greatest of the Hindu dynasties that ruled India, the Guptas.

The Golden Gupta Era

Four Gupta monarchs, Chandragupta, Samudragupta, Chandragupta II (also known as Vikramaditya) and Kumargupta were based originally in Magadha (Bihar). At the height of their power they had the Indo-Gangetic plain, down to the northern fringes of the Deccan, under their control. They and their descendants ruled for over three centuries – from AD 300 up to the death of Harsha in AD 647. Two Chinese travellers, Fa Hsien, who spent nine years (AD 401-10) during the reign of Chandragupta II, and Hieun Tsang, who spent over thirty years (AD 635-64) during the reign of Harsha, have left glowing accounts of what they saw in India. The latter account is confirmed by the Indian court-poet, Bana.

The three centuries of Gupta dominance are known in Indian history as the Golden Age of the Guptas. Peace and stability provided by the succession of monarchs saw the blossoming of art and literature to its fullness. The somewhat crude argotish Pali was replaced by the highly polished and grammar-perfect Sanskrit. It was in Sanskrit that the great poets and dramatists, Kalidasa (AD 350-460), Bhartrihari and Bhavabhuti (eighth century AD), Amaru and Sudraka wrote and recited. Never again did Sanskrit literature attain the same heights of literary excellence.

Hindu scholars were not as insular then as they became later. The astronomer, Varahamihira, (AD 587), introduced Greek science into India. Indians invented the all-important concept of zero and algebra. They made advances in the study of astronomy and were able to forecast eclipses and the conjunctions of stars with uncanny accuracy. It is from the Hindus that the Arabs gained this knowledge.

Hindu *Vedanta* was taken further with the proliferation of schools of philosophy. Painting, sculpture (e.g., Ajanta and Ellora) and the crafts developed astonishing styles of beauty. Casting of bronze and mixing of different metals became a pastime. The iron pillar of Delhi is a living tribute to the Gupta metallurgists. It has withstood the elements for 2000 years without rusting. Even cannon-balls made no more than a dent in its sides.

It is no small wonder that Hinduism and Hindu culture spread from India to Burma, Sri Lanka, Indonesia, Bali, Cambodia, Thailand and Vietnam. The ruins of Borobudur and Angkor Vat are Hindu in concept and execution.

In the Vedas, the Upanishads and the Gita we have glimpses of the excellence of the language in which those hymns and philosophic concepts were rendered. We also have some examples of secular works executed at about the same time. There are the *Panchatantra* tales from which Aesop's fables took their form and content. There is the widely circulating work on sex, *Kama Sutra*, ascribed to Vatsyayan. There are many others devoted to medicine, astronomy, astrology, music and dance.

A creative people, with a limited supply of writing material, concentrated more on poetry and drama, which could be memorised, than on novels. And it is in the compositions of these later poets that we see Sanskrit at its best. The examples cited here are taken from an admirable translation by John Brough (*Poems from the Sanskrit*, Penguin).

India's early poets, like their counterparts in other countries, were given to moralising.

Patience, better than armour, guards from harm
And why seek enemies, if you have anger?

Admonishes Bhartrihari and advises the King:

Prince, would you milk this bounteous cow, the state?
First, you must let the people drink their share:
Only when calves are fed, will earth's tree bear
Fruit, like cornucopia for your plate.

The besetting sin of hubris evoked this from Sudraka's pen:

The cure for pride is knowledge. Who can cure
A man who's proud of knowledge? If the patient
Should be allergic to ambrosia,
The prognosis
Is hopeless.

Sudraka praised the generous spender, not oddly enough, the philanthrop:

The open-handed have the tighter fist:
They take their hoarded merits when they go.
The man is your philanthropist:
When dead he leaves his total wealth below.

Aphorisms were always popular in the Orient. They,

like the following example, again from Sudraka, pithily summed up banal platitudes:

A book, a woman, and money-loan,
Once they are gone, are gone.
And better so – sometimes they do return
piecemeal; or soiled; or torn.

Jayadeva excelled in his admonitory verse:

Shun these six faults to win success:
Sleep, sloth,
Fear, wrath,
Slovenliness, long-windedness.

And, says Jayadeva, avoid the following:

A teacher failing in his moral teaching,
A priest unscholarly who's still preaching,
A king whose subjects look for help in vain,
A wife whose voice portends a husband's pain,
A shepherd who on urban pleasures broods,
A barber dreaming of the hills and woods,
All six – avoid them. Everyone can be
As lethal as a leaky boat at sea.

Moralising seldom produces great poetry. Nor did it extract the best from the poets we have quoted. Preoccupation with time and death drew some beautiful lines from Bhartrihari. He mourned:

The night that's pass will not return to me
The Jumna's floods flow onward to the sea.

And again:

The pleasant city and its mighty king,
Tributary princes at his side,
The learned men that were the kingdom's pride,
The gracious ladies of the court, the ring
Of haughty nobles, arrogant of birth.
Are conquered by the Lord of all the earth,
Time, who makes memories of everything.

Bhartrihari regretted the short span of human life:

A man lives long who lives a hundred years:
Yet half is sleep, and half the rest again
Old age and childhood. For the rest, a man
Lives close companion to disease and tears,
Losing his love, working for other men.
Where can joy find a space in this short span?

Poverty, old age, desolation and death are recurring
themes, Amaru's description of an old man is
memorable.

At dawn the old man, slowly, painfully,
Managed to stand, but trembling at the knees,
Clutching hard-fist over stick, while tears meet
The dribble from the corner of his mouth,
His scorched and fragment rags barely concealing
A tattered lion-cloth. Forcing crooked legs

> To give their utmost paralytic speed,
> He started on another day's long road,
> Shivering, half-conscious of the bitter wind.

Yogeswara's portrayal of a scene of desolation is reminiscent of Goldsmith's deserted village:

> Still in the hamlets of this wretched land
> Some families exist, though thinned and torn
> By hard oppression of a landlord's hand,
> Yet loath to leave the homes where they were born.
> And now the mongoose wanders where he will
> Where only broken thatch and walls remain;
> From their pale, liquid throats, the pigeons still
> Murmur with beauty, to assuage the pain.

And this memorable description of famine by Dharmakirti:

> Hand in clasped hand and side pressed close to side,
> Silently stand some children of the poor,
> And shyly, hungry eyes half turned aside,
> Observe the eater through the open door.

The Sanskrit poet excelled in describing the beauty of nature, a faculty which eluded the succeeding generations of India's poets and is virtually unknown to contemporary poets. Much of this nature poetry was occasioned by the spectacular arrival of the monsoon after months of searing heat. Bhartrihari sums up the experience:

The summer sun, who robbed the pleasant nights,
And plundered all the water of the rivers,
And burned the earth, and scorched the forest trees,
Is now in hiding; and the autumn clouds,
Spread thick across the sky to track him down,
Hunt for the criminal with lightning flashes.

The monsoon is the time for love. So said Sudraka's
maiden to the thundercloud on her way to her tryst:

Thundercloud, I think you are wicked.
You know I'm going to meet my own lover,
And yet you first scare me with your thunder,
And now you're trying to caress me
With your rain-hands.

Sudraka caught the fragrance of the rain-soaked
night:

Black clouds at midnight,
Deep thunder rolling.
The night has lost the moon,
A cow lowing for her lost calf.

Amaru's heart went out to the young husband
separated from his bride during the season of the rains:

At night the rain came, and the thunder deep
Rolled in the distance; and he could not sleep,
But tossed and turned, with long and frequent sighs,
And as he listened, tears came to his eyes;
And thinking of his young wife left alone,

He sobbed and wept aloud till dawn.
And from that time on
The villagers made it a strict rule that no traveller
Should be allowed to take a room
For the night in the village.

The monsoon was not all that roused these men to poetic frenzy. Note Sudraka's description of the deepening twilight and the similarity with Gray's *Elegy* penned a thousand years later:

Slowly the darkness drains away the sunlight.
Drawn homeward to their nests, the crows fall silent.
And now the owl sits in the hollow tree,
Bolder, neck sunk inside his body,
And stares; swivels his head; and stares.

The erotic has always been the Indian poets' *forte*. Some of it is in the oriental tradition, more facetious than beautiful. Thus wrote Bhartrihari about a wanton wench displaying her treasures:

On sunny days there in the shade
Beneath the trees reclined a maid
Who lifted up her dress (she said)
To keep the moonbeams off her head.

Rajashekhara's catalogue of a woman's beauty preceded Shakespeare's by many centuries:

This is her face? Then the moon's tale is told.
And this her lustre? Then alas for gold.

The lotus is made worthless by her eyes,
All nectar's virtues her sweet smile supplies.
When set beside her brows, what is love's bow?
That the Creator does not plagiarise
His own fair works, these fair examples show.

And this as an example of Bhartrihari's moralising:

In this vain fleeting universe, a man
Of wisdom has two courses: first, he can
Direct his time to pray, to save his soul,
And wallow in religion's nectar-bowl;
But, if he cannot, it surely best,
To touch and hold a lovely woman's breast;
And to caress her warm, round hips and thighs,
And to possess that which between them lies.

Bhartrihari could at times be more explicitly erotic:

No! don't! she says at first, while she-despises
The very thought of love; then she reveals
A small desire; and passion soon arises,
Shyly at first, but in the end she yields.
With confidence then playing without measure
Love's secret game, at last no more afraid
She spreads her legs wide in her boundless
pleasure.
Ah! love is lovely with a lovely maid!

Sometimes Bhartrihari descended to the level of
an adolescent scribble on the lavatory wall:

Khajuraho

Burning from Shiva's wrath, the god of love
Plunged in the lake between my lady's thighs
To quench the flames; and hence as smoke arises
The curling hairs on Venus's mount above.

Bhavabhuti is more subtle in handling the same
theme:

The lamps were lit and the night far spent,
And he, my love, was on love intent
And he knew full well just what loving meant:
Though he made his love in a cautious way

The wretched bed upon which we lay
Creaked, and had far too much to say.

The most famous of the ancient writers was
Kalidasa. He was primarily a dramatist. His best known
play is *Shakuntala*. Many English translations of this
and the romantic dramatised tale *Vikramorvashi* and
Meghduta – The Cloud Messenger – are available.

The Empire of the Guptas disintegrated in much
the same manner as other empires before theirs. Once
more the sluice gates in the north-west were forced
open and India was inundated by rude, barbaric tribes
of vandals from Central Asia. For 500 years the White
Huns (Mongols) created so much chaos that no record
remains save that of destruction – the burning of
Taxila, desecration of Buddhist temples and
monasteries in Afghanistan and the Punjab.

Following the Huns came other tribes of whom we
know little besides their names: Gurjaras, Maitrakas,
Jats, Aheers, Rajputs; they settled down in the Indo-
Gangetic plain to farm and raise cattle. Brahmanical
Hinduism was still flexible enough to accommodate
them in the caste hierarchy: The Rajputs were made
Kshatriyas, other tribes, Sudras. It is believed that
some small tribes of emigrants were even accepted as
Brahmins.

Significant changes took place in the social system.
The Hindus did not permit widows to remarry. The
most numerous of the new emigrant tribes, the Jats,

did and continued to do so even after their conversion to Hinduism. The Rajputs, however, zealously pursued the awful customs of burning widows (*sati*) on the funeral pyres of their husbands and *jauhar*, mass suicide by women following the defeat and death of their menfolk in battle.

It should be noted that although the new tribes settled in the Indo-Gangetic plains, readjustments in the caste structure started in the north and were extended to the Dravidians in the south. The one significant difference between the northern and southern cast systems was the predominance of the Kshatriyas and Vaishyas in the north and their virtual non-existence in the south.

11

Advent of Islam

*T*he Muslim conquest of India had the most profound impact on the political, social and cultural life of the country.

Islam came to India before the Muslim conquerors. Arab traders brought Islam to the western coast within a few years of the death of the Prophet. Then in AD 712 the seventeen-year-old Mohammed Bin Qasim invaded Sindh. This incursion was, however, as the celebrated historian Lane Poole remarked, "an episode in the history of India and Islam, a triumph without results". One might qualify that remark by saying that it did have one result, it showed the Muslims that India was rich and easy to conquer.

It took the Muslims another two centuries before they could mount a full-scale invasion of India. This was left to Mahmud of Ghazni. Between AD 1000 and AD 1027, i.e., in twenty-seven years he invaded India seventeen times. He decimated Hindu opposition, destroyed Hindu temples and sacked Hindu cities along the Jumna and the Ganges. His most spectacular victory was on his sixteenth invasion when he crossed the Sindh desert and captured the holy city of Somnath on the Arabian Sea. He destroyed this great temple and carried enormous wealth back with him. Ever since, the name Mahmud has stunk in the nostrils of the Hindus – and the rebuilding of Somnath attained symbolic significance for them.

Mahmud struck terror in the hearts of Indians. The historian, Ibn Zafir, records that following an Indian custom entitling a victorious raja to cut a finger off his vanquished foe, Mahmud collected a hoard of severed fingers before he left India. However, with savagery towards the infidel, Mahmud combined sophistication and patronage of the arts and literature. One of the greatest poets of the Persian language, Firdausi, lived in his court. So did the historian Al Beruni.

Mahmud's violence and vandalism brought the Hindu rajas together. His last incursion in AD 1027 had to be cut short; the Indians harassed him and then halted his advance on the banks of the Indus. No sooner had Mahmud turned his back than they re-established control. For the next 150 years northern India was ruled by the Rajputs: Chauhans at Ajmer and

Delhi, Parmars at Malwa; Rathors, Kacchawas, Bundelas and Tomaras in other regions.

The real conqueror-founder of the Islamic empire in India was Mohammed Ghori. His first invasion in AD 1175 brought him as far as Multan. His second attempt was thwarted, but in his third and fourth invasions he overran most of the Punjab. Then he came up against united Indian opposition, led by the Rajput chief, Prithvi Raj Chauhan. In the battle of Tarain, fought in 1191, the Rajputs defeated the invaders. If the poet, Chand Bardai, is to be believed, Prithvi Raj worsted Ghori in personal combat and, as a chivalrous Rajput, allowed him to go free. For this act of magnanimity Indians paid a heavy price. The next year Mohammed Ghori came back on the very same battlefield of Tarain, defeated and slew Prithvi Raj. Ghori's Viceroy, Qutubuddin Aibak, who later succeeded him as Sultan, captured Delhi and Mathura and the territories between the Jumna and the Ganges. A contemporary historian has recorded: "Temples were converted to mosques and abodes of goodness; and the ejaculations of bead-counters and the voices of the muezzins ascended to the highest heaven. The very name of idolatry was annihilated ... 50,000 men came under the collar of slavery and the plains became as black as pitch with Hindus."

Thereafter, the invaders took on other Rajput chieftains in turn and eliminated them one by one. The ease with which Muslim invaders went through

India is scarcely credible. A Muslim general, Bakhtiyar Khilji, conquered Bihar in 1193, destroyed Buddhist *viharas*, massacred Buddhist monks or forced them to flee to Nepal or Tibet. Six years later, he pushed on into Bengal. According to legend, when an advance party of ten Turkish horsemen arrived at Nadia, the capital of Bengal, the King, Lakshmana Sen, fled by boat.

Mohammed Ghori did not spend very much time in India. But his slaves, whom he appointed as Viceroys, consolidated his conquests and set up what came to be known as the dynasty of slave sultans. First there was Qutubuddin, a generous tyrant who bestowed by the hundred thousand and slaughtered by the hundred thousand (*lakh-baksh*). He was followed by Iltutmish (1210-35) who was succeeded for a brief period of three and a half years by his daughter Razia Sultana (1236-40). The slave dynasty declined after Ghiyasuddin Balban (1286) who ruled northern India with an iron hand for forty years.

Before we go into the next Muslim dynasty it might be profitable to know why Hindu India crumbled so easily before the Muslim onslaught.

The most decisive cause of Hindu defeat was Hindu disunity. Hindus were always eager to see their own enemies destroyed even if they knew that their own destruction would follow as a matter of course. This led to the defeat of Prithvi Raj, and then of his rival, Raja Jai Chand. Even in the field of battle, the Hindus would not have a unified command and fought under their respective chieftains. Desertion by one chief became a rout.

The Hindu's caste distinctions only allowed a small proportion of the population, the Kshatriyas, to wield arms. The rest of the people remained spectators, often indifferent to the fate that befell the arrogant "warrior caste".

The Hindu technique of warfare did not match the Muslim. Their commanders rode on elephants; their footmen were

Qutub Minar, Delhi

armed with lances or maces. Muslims rode swift-footed horses and had archers. The elephants of the Hindus frequently turned back to trample their own forces while Muslim archers carried out heavy slaughter from a safe distance.

The Turk, Mongol, Afghan and Persian soldiers were bigger, stronger and better motivated than their Hindu adversaries. The Muslim was at once a crescentader fired with fanatic zeal to destroy the infidel and a freebooter intent on bettering his lot by the wealth of Hindustan.

Let us return to the succession of Muslim dynasties.

The slave-sultans were followed by another Turkish dynasty, the Khiljis. By now the rulers had to fight on two fronts: one, against the Indians and the other against Mongol tribesmen, who had begun to knock at the north-western gates of India. The most distinguished of the Khilji monarchs was Alauddin who ruled for twenty years (1296-1316). His general, Malik Kafur, conquered the Deccan and then the whole of South India by 1312 – thus justifying the title his master had assumed for himself *Sikandar-i-Sani* (Alexander II).

The Khiljis gave way to another Turkish dynasty, the Tughlaks, who ruled for seventy years from 1320-97. Their greatest king was the eccentric Mohammed Tughlak who ruled (1325-51) an empire almost as large as that of Alauddin Khilji. He experimented with two capitals, one at Delhi and the other in the Deccan at Daulatabad and introduced token currency – an experiment which drained his treasury of all its gold and silver. Although he raised new kinds of taxes, he was not unduly harsh towards his Hindu subjects and even married Hindu wives.

Mohammed's successor, Firuze, who ruled for thirty-seven years (1351-88), was a builder of cities and waterways as well as a patron of learning. But Tughlak decline also began in the days of Firuze. The ruler and the aristocracy began to indulge themselves. Firuze had as many as 180,000 slaves to serve him. One of his ministers, Khan Jahan Maqbul, a Hindu convert to Islam, is said to have had 2,000 women of different nationalities in his harem.

The last effective ruler of the Tughlak dynasty, Nasiruddin, was unable to withstand the onslaught of the Mongol tribes. In 1397 Taimur (Tamerlane to the Europeans) crossed the Indus into India. He was not the first of his tribe to dream of an empire. Chenghiz Khan (1227) had spread Mongol power from the Persian Gulf to the Dneiper and in 1258 Hulagu Khan had sacked Baghdad, the seat of the Islamic Caliphate.

Taimur (1336-1405) carried the sword of expansion further afield. At the time he came into India, his tribesmen were extracting tax and loot from countries ranging from the Mediterranean to China. "My object in the invasion of Hindustan is to lead an expedition against the infidel," he recorded, "to purify the land from the filth of infidelity and polytheism; and that we may overthrow their temples and idols and become *Ghazis* and *Mujahids* before Allah."

He more than justified the title of *Ghazi*. Before engaging the armies of the Sultan of Delhi, Taimur ordered the massacre of 100,000 Hindu prisoners taken in the Punjab campaign. This was to prevent their rising against him on the eve of the battle. Thus, "the sword of Islam was washed in the blood of infidels" and many Hindus terrorised into accepting Islam as, for instance, the Raja of Jammu, of whom it is recorded that "by hopes, fears and threats he was brought to see the beauty of Islam. He repeated the creed, ate the flesh of the cow, which is an abomination – and so obtained honour – and protection of the Emperor".

No one could withstand Taimur. After plundering the Punjab he ransacked Delhi for fifteen days. For northern India, Taimur was verily the scourge of Allah, for he left nothing except "anarchy, pestilence and famine behind him". The immediate effect of his invasion was to break up India into two: the northern half was recovered by the Turks and the Afghans: the Saiyyads (1414-47) and the Lodhis (1447-1526) ruled parts of northern India from Delhi. The south became independent under Hindu kings.

The end of the fifteenth century is an appropriate time to make a balance sheet of the achievements and failures of the 500 years of Muslim presence in India.

Islam had certainly gained a firm foothold in the country. But it was not the massacres and the destruction of innumerable temples which gained it converts. Forcible conversions were, as they usually are, for a short duration. Moreover, violence was repaid by violence: as soon as Muslim power weakened, Hindus wreaked vengeance on the Muslims. The majority of early Muslims were, in fact, Turks, Afghans, Persians and Arabs who came with the invading armies, found Indian wives and made their homes in India. With these Muslim communities as the nucleus, Islam spread amongst Hindu tribes – sometimes because of the political influence of the Muslims, more often through the proselytisation of Mullahs, especially the Sufi mystics. Most of the converts were Hindus of the lower castes. They could no longer turn to Buddhism:

there were no Buddhists left to turn to; their only escape from persecution by the upper castes was Islam. It would appear that clans and villages were converted *en masse*. Thus many tribes of Rajputs and Jats in the Punjab and villages in East Bengal became Muslim.

Few people combined the creator-destroyer aspect of God as effectively as did the Muslim conquerors of India. Since temples were to them idolatrous abominations, they destroyed what must have been works of great beauty executed by sculptors and painters over many decades of hard work. The little that remains of the Buddhist frescoes inside the caves of Bamiyan in Afghanistan – and of the disfigured monoliths outside – is breathtaking in the grandeur of design and dimension. The Turks made a thorough job of destruction in the Indo-Gangetic plain. But even so the remains of the twenty-seven Rajput temples in Delhi, the carvings on the pillars, damaged torsos and limbs of Hindu gods and goddesses that excavations have yielded show the high degree of skill attained and the religious fanaticism that made the conquering Turks turn a blind eye to things of beauty.

Muslims were forbidden to reproduce likeness of living creatures as that amounted to usurping the functions of Allah. So Muslim artists turned to calligraphy and floral designs. Copies of the Quran, memoirs, and verses were reproduced in stylised lettering in black ink, silver and gold; margins embellished with leaves and flowers. Muslim sculptors reproduced the various styles of calligraphy and floral motifs in stone and alabaster.

Amongst the earliest examples of their art is the *Quwwat-ul-Islam* ("Might of Islam") mosque raised over the ruins of the Rajput temples at Delhi and the beautiful 293-foot tower, the Qutub Minar (began by Qutubuddin Aibak and completed by Iltutmish). In the great mosque we have Moorish arches, often over a hundred feet high, festooned with verses from the Quran in *Nashkh* and *Kufic* styles going up and across like a flowering creeper.

The tomb of Iltutmish, at the same site, and of his son, Sultan Ghori, a few miles from the Qutub Minar, are other examples of Turkish art and architecture. A replica of the *Quwwat-ul-Islam* mosque stands in Ajmer: the *adhai din ka jhonpra* (hut-built-in-2 ½ days) presumably referring to the speed with which it was executed.

It would appear that though the invaders brought their own architects and draftsmen, the works were executed by Hindu craftmen, stone-cutters and builders. And where details had not been prescribed by Muslim architects, these Hindu workers filled them in with objects familiar to them and which did not offend Muslim susceptibilities. Thus the lotus flower was used as a plaque to inscribe in name of Allah, the elephant trunk raised in salute as an emblem of royalty; even the temple bell found a mute *entrée* on the pillars of Muslim mosques and mausoleums.

Hindu influence insinuated itself further in the buildings erected by the Khiljis and the Tughlaks. Of the Khiljis we have the Alai Darwaza alongside the Qutub Minar and the Jamaat Khana mosque beside the tomb of the Sufi, Nizamuddin, in present-day New Delhi. Little now remains of the *Qasr-i-hazar satoon* ("the palace of a thousand pillars") at Siri, also in New Delhi, or of the *Jahan-panah* ("refuge of the world") fort of the Tughlaks. But contemporary historians have recorded their grandeur in glowing terms.

The tomb of Ghiyasuddin Tughlak and the Begampuri mosque of Mohammed Tughlak indicate attempts to shed Hindu influence and reproduce the austere, bold and powerful architecture of Central Asia. For a time this style became the vogue with the greatest builder of the Tughlaks, Firoze, who raised several cities, *madrassahs* (seminaries), mosques and mausoleums. With Firoze we also see the bourgeoning of the bulbous dome, striking in its sensuous likeness to the female breast – and the re-emergence of Hindu motifs: the lotus flower imprinted with the name of Allah, the corbel disguised as an elephant trunk and often the ornate temple bell now looking like a suspended beehive.

The hand of the Hindu craftsman becomes even more evident in the designs of the tombs and mosques of the Saiyad and Lodhi kings. The female-breasted dome attained perfection with the Lodhis (The *bara gumbad* of Sikandar Lodhi and the domes of tombs in the Lodhi gardens in New Delhi are superb examples). Even the master-builders of the Mughals were unable to reproduce the sinuous outlines of the Lodhis' domes.

Kings were patrons of scholars and poets, most of whom were refugees from Muslim countries terrorised by the Mongols. They wrote in Turkish, Arabic or Persian and disdained the languages of Hindustan. By then Hindu scholars had also closed their minds to everything alien – and to them anything Muslim was alien. Al Baruni who came to India in the eleventh century (with the notorious Mahmud of Ghazni) was struck by the arrogant insularity of Brahmin scholars. "Their haughtiness is such that if you tell them of any science or scholar in Khorasan or Persia, they will think you both an ignoramus and a liar." He dismissed all pandits as a pack of fools and wrote: "Folly is an illness against which there is no medicine." The little that he gleaned of Hindu scholarship filled him with revulsion because it appeared to him to be mixed up with superstition and magic. Al Beruni rejected Indian astronomy and astrology as a mixture of pearls with sour dates and turd.

There were other Muslim scholars and historians: Qazi Minhajuddin Siraj (thirteenth century), Ziauddin Barani (author of *Tarikh-i-Firozeshahi* and the "History of Balban and his Successors"), Shams Siraj Afifi and Yahya bin Ahmed (*Tarikh-i-Mubarak Shahi*). There were also many poets, but the most outstanding being Abul

Hassan and Amir Khusrau (1253-1325) who was honoured with the title *Toot-i-Hind* ("the Nightingale of India"). Although most of his works were in Persian, he was amongst the first of the Muslim poets to start composing verses in Hindi. This was probably due to the influence of the Sufi, Nizamuddin Auliya, whose disciple he became. Khusrau was a many-sided genius: courtier (he served seven rulers), soldier, Sufi, poet and musician, he is said to have invented the sitar as well as some *ragas* of Indian music. He is best known for many of his rhyming riddles which are popular amongst children to this day. These riddles pun on Indian words and are therefore very difficult to translate into another language. However, here is an attempt to render the one most commonly quoted:

> Twenty I sliced, cut off their heads
> No life was lost, no blood was shed.

The answer is contained in the lines: the two words *na khoon* ("no blood"). When joined together into one word, *nakhoon* means nails; the answer being, paring of the nails.

Some of Khusrau's riddles are not for children. This one for instance has an amorous *double entendre*.

> All night he stayed up with me.
> Came the dawn and out he went.
> His going did my heart repent
> Ho friend! you think 'twas my lover?
> No friend, the oil in the lamp was spent.

Khusrau came to love India, its arts, its music, its mangoes and its betel-leaf. In his writings one sees the conflict of man trying to reconcile his ancestral legacy of Muslim superiority with the ethos of the land of his domicile.

The death anniversary (*urs*) of Amir Khusrau is a great event in Delhi where he is buried a few yards away from the tomb of Nizamuddin, the saint he worshipped. Here, all through the night, parties of *qawwals* sing his compositions: some in praise of the Prophet (*nat-i-rasul*), some in praise of his peer and religious mentor, Nizamuddin, and some in praise of his country – India.

12

The Mughals

*T*he Mughals ruled India for two hundred years leaving a deep and everlasting impression on the method of administration, art, architecture, literature, music, manners and way of living of the peoples of the country. A succession of six monarchs, each remarkable in his own way, helped to write the most glorious chapter in the history of India. Even in their decline, when they suffered rebellious upstarts, the Mughal kings commanded the respect and affection of their erstwhile subjects. The dynasty ended in a bloodbath which to this day brings tears to the eyes of the people.

The Mughal saga had a gory beginning. Indians had heard of the terrible doings of Chenghiz and Hulagu Khan. For over a century, savage Mongol tribes had knocked at India's northwestern gates and often succeeded in forcing an entry. In 1398 Taimur had muscled his way in and given northern India a taste of the medicine that the Mongols gave to those who dared to stand in their way.

For a hundred years India had remained in a state of traumatic shock. The Indo-Gangetic plain, Maharashtra, Gujarat and the Deccan were broken up into many principalities where Muslim chieftains assumed royal titles. Rajputs asserted their independence in Rajasthan, Hindu rajas in Orissa, and in the south the kings of Vijaynagar set up a powerful monarchy of their own.

Babar (1526-30)

"I never ceased to think of the conquest of Hindustan," wrote Babar in his *Memoirs*. He had convinced himself that as a descendant of Chenghiz, Hulagu and Taimur he had a right to conquer India. His ambitions were fired by stories he heard of India's wealth.

Babar

Babar overcame his enemies in his native Samarkand, advanced eastwards through Afghanistan into India. In the course of seven years from 1519 to 1526 he entered India five times. From the very first, Babar came determined to stay. "Do not hurt or harm the flocks or herds of these people ..." he warned his soldiers. "Possession of this country by a Turk has come down from of old; beware not to bring ruin on its people by giving way to fear or anxiety; our eye is on this land and on this people; raid and rapine shall not be." This was said in 1519 when he was on his second expedition and in occupation of much of north-western Punjab.

The next year when Babar came back to the Punjab he sensed that disputes between different branches of the Lodhi Afghans (one of whom ruled over Delhi) could be exploited to his advantage. After a pause of four years Babar re-entered India, and having subjugated the Punjab, made preparations to advance on Delhi. He wrote in his *Memoirs:* "On Friday, November 17, AD 1525, when the sun was in Sagittarius, I set out on my march to invade Hindustan ... putting my foot in the stirrup of resolution, and taking in my hands the reins of faith, I marched against Sultan Ibrahim, son of Sultan Sikandar, son of Sultan Bahlol Lodhi Afghan, in whose possession the city of Delhi and Kingdom of Hindustan at that time were."

Babar's adversary Ibrahim Lodhi was a man of limited ability. By his arrogance he had forfeited the support of his Afghan kinsmen. "Kings have no kin," he had proclaimed somewhat haughtily. Although he was able to muster 100,000 men to oppose the 10,000 Mughals under Babar's command, not many in his host had stomach for battle. The issue was settled on the morning of the twenty-first of April 1526, on the field of Panipat. Babar's superior tactics – the deployment of cavalry against lines of chained elephants and, above all, the use of artillery – won him a decisive victory in six brief hours. By noon 20,000 of the Lodhi army, including Sultan Ibrahim, were slain and the remainder in full retreat. Babar did not give them time to regroup. He sent his son, Humayun, on to take Agra, while he himself marched to occupy Delhi.

The capture of Delhi and Agra (Humayun obtained the fabled Koh-i-noor diamond at Agra) did not bring the rest of northern India to heel. Though Babar exhorted the Indians not to "fly from our conquest", but make terms with it, the Rajputs banded together in a determined effort to expel him from the country. They were led by Rana Sanga whose body bore marks of his martial exploits: he had lost an arm and an eye and had eighty scars on his person.

On the sixteenth of March, 1527 a very nervous Babar, forswearing wine and calling upon Allah to help him in a holy war against the infidel, clashed with the Rajputs at Kanhua, thirty miles from Agra. Once more Babar was victorious. He expressed his gratitude to the Lord of Hosts by raising a mound of Rajput skulls, investing himself with the title of *ghazi* (slayer of infidels) and getting gloriously drunk.

After the victory at Kanhua, Babar and his sons took other provinces piecemeal. In the winter of 1527-28 he captured Chanderi fortress, then Kanauj, and finally Ranthambor. In the spring of 1528 he drove the Afghans along the Ganges, further eastwards; his second son, Askari, penetrated deeper into Bengal. Thus in four short years Babar made himself master of most of northern India.

Babar had come to stay. But he liked neither India nor the Indians. "Three things oppressed us in India," he wrote, "heat, violent winds, dust." And in another memorable passage, he denounced almost everything he saw: "… a country naturally full of charm but its inhabitants are devoid of grace; and in intercourse with them there is neither friendly society, amity or stable relationship. They have no genius, no comprehension, no politeness, no generosity, no robustness of feeling. In their ideas, as in their ways of production, they lack method, art, rules and theory. There are no baths, candles, torches, schools or even candlesticks."

The only things Babar praised of India were the countryside, its monsoon – and its gold. Having savoured the first two and acquired much of the third, he longed for the cool, fragrant air of his homeland and the watermelons of Kabul.

According to legend, Babar brought death upon himself. When his elder son was taken ill and pronounced beyond cure by doctors, Babar circled his son's bed three times repeating, "O God! If a life be exchanged for a life, I who am Babar give my life and my being for Humayun … I have borne it away." And so it was: Humayun rose from his sick bed, Babar was stricken with fever. After expressing his wish to be buried in Kabul, the last words he spoke were "Lord, I am here with Thee."

Babar died at the age of forty-eight. He was buried in a garden *aramgah* (resting-place) which he had laid out on the western bank of the river Jumna at Agra. Fourteen years later his remains were taken to Kabul.

Humayun (1530-56); Sher Shah Suri (1540-45)

Humayun was twenty-three years old when he inherited Babar's kingdom. He was temperamentally unfit to rule the empire his doting father had bequeathed to him. He was of a scholarly bent of mind and enjoyed reading classics in the languages he knew: Turkish, Persian, Arabic and Hindi. He studied mathematics, philosophy, astronomy and astrology. He had no stomach for intrigue or flattery; he wanted to be left alone. His father had often chided him: "Indolence and laziness accord not at all with the exercise of sovereignty."

Babar had arranged to have him trained in the art of administration, made him Governor of Badakshan and later of districts of the Punjab. But it was obvious that Humayun could not make up his mind between being a king and a scholar. His father loaded the scales against him. Although he recognised Humayun as his heir, he gave his other three sons large tracts which, in effect, divided and weakened the Empire. And he did not effectively weaken the Afghans who began to reassert their power in different regions. While Humayun was dallying at Agra or occupied in building

Din Panah, a suburb of Delhi, Afghan chieftains, notably Sher Shah Suri, began to consolidate their power in Bihar and Bengal. Humayun moved against Sher Shah Suri. Sher Shah Suri retreated, then turned round and cut off Humayun's contact with his capital. Meanwhile, one of Humayun's brothers proclaimed himself Emperor of Hindustan.

Sher Shah Suri awaited the monsoon. Then on 26 June 1539, at Chausa, he fell upon Humayun's army, marooned in the rain-sogged country and slew 8,000 Mughals. Humayun escaped by swimming across a river with a handful of companions. Sher Shah Suri pursued him all the way to Agra and into the Punjab. Menaced by his brother's postures, Humayun fled through the Sindh deserts out of Hindustan.

For the next five years (1540-45) till he died, Sher Shah Suri was Emperor of India. Few men have left so lasting an impression of their administrative genius in so short a time as did this Afghan commoner who had risen to become a king. His able minister, Todar Mal, organised the revenue system of India (the tax varied between one-third to a quarter of the yield according to the capacity of the land) which continued right into the British period. Sher Shah linked the major cities of northern India with roads, lined them with trees, built rest-houses for travellers and abolished tolls which used to be levied by villages and towns on merchandise passing through them. He raised his Hindu employees into positions of eminence and recruited Rajputs in his army. For the five years he ruled there was peace in the land. No one knew or cared for the fate of Humayun. Some historians have described Sher Shah Suri

Humayun Tomb, Delhi

as the "greatest of the Muslim rulers of India" (Sir W. Haig). Sher Shah was killed when a mine exploded while he was besieging a fort.

Sher Shah Suri's successors – first his son Islam Shah (1545-53) and, on his death, Islam's son Firoze (murdered three days after his accession) and finally, Sher Shah's brother, Adil Shah Suri – were unable to hold the domain together.

By 1556 there were four independent Afghan kingdoms and the most powerful man was a Hindu bania shopkeeper, Hemu, who ruled Delhi in the name of his Suri patron. In the latter years the monsoons were poor; there was famine, and following the famine an epidemic.

The Persians helped Humayun to return to India. Once again the fate of India was decided on the field of Panipat. On 5 November 1556 Humayun clashed with Hemu's vast army of 1,500 war elephants and an assortment of horse and foot. The elephants panicked; Hemu was hit in the eye by a stray arrow and was deserted by his host.

Humayun quickly proceeded to reoccupy Delhi and Agra. A few weeks later, he heard the call for prayer come up from a minaret of a neighbouring mosque built by Sher Shah Suri. Humayun hurried down. He missed his footing (Muslim architects were notoriously inept in the design of their steps) and fractured his skull. Thus ended the short and interrupted rule of one described by an eminent historian as "the problem child of the Mughals" (T.G.P. Spear).

Akbar (1556-1605)

Humayun's son, Jalaluddin Akbar, was a rootless child. He was born on the full moon of the night of 23 November 1542 in the desert fortress of Amarkot when his parents were fleeing from India. The best that his father could offer to those who came to felicitate him were the contents of a pod of musk ("This is all the present I can afford to make you on the birth of my son, whose fame will, I trust, be one day expanded all over the world, as the perfume of the

Akbar

musk now fills this apartment"). He was nursed by a foster-mother but had no one to teach him how to read and write. He spent his boyhood flying pigeons and hunting. Like his father and grandfather, he was endowed with a powerful physique, a sharp mind and an excellent memory which enabled him to recite works of poets like Hafiz and Rumi by heart.

When his father stumbled down to his death, Akbar was a wayward lad of fourteen. He was proclaimed Emperor of Hindustan but the power behind the Mughal throne was a kinsman, Bairam Khan. Bairam Khan was an awesome man; he made the boy, Akbar, flesh his sword in the body of the dying Hemu. Bairam Khan became drunk with power. It took young Akbar four years to get rid of him. For another two years the state was administered by his foster-mother and her son, Adham Khan. Akbar spent these years hunting tigers and elephants. Adham Khan led the Mughal armies in many victorious campaigns. He roused his master's ire by taking more than his share of the loot and the women and by murdering a minister whom he suspected of being a rival. Akbar had Adham Khan hurled from the ramparts of the fort of Delhi. At twenty he became Emperor of Hindustan, both in name and in fact.

In the year 1562 when Akbar came into his own inheritance, he launched an experiment to make his subjects, both Muslim and Hindu, into one nation. He set an example by taking a Hindu wife and raising her Rajput kinsmen to positions of eminence. The alliance brought him into personal contact with Hinduism. He was already inclined towards Sufism and developed a revulsion towards zealots who claimed to have the sole monopoly of the truth. His diarist records him as

INDIA

UNDER-AKBAR (1605)

having said: "On the completion of my twentieth year, I experienced an internal bitterness, and from the lack of spiritual provision for my last journey my soul was seized with exceeding sorrow..."

The following year Akbar ordered the abolition of tax on Hindus going on pilgrimages and followed it up by repealing the tax paid by them in lieu of military service (*jiziya*).

Akbar then proceeded to subdue the entire country. "A monarch should be ever intent on conquest, otherwise his neighbours rise in arms against him," he said.

In quick succession he moved against recalcitrant elements among the Rajputs (1567), humbled the Sisodias, Rathors and Chauhans and then brought the whole of Uttar Pradesh (1569), Gujarat (1572) and Bengal (1574-76) under his domain. The only people to put up stiff resistance were the Rajputs. Much as Akbar tried to win them over by further matrimonial alliances and offers of service, the hard core led by the Sisodias under Rana Pratap of Udaipur, refused to submit or make terms.

Akbar had to put down rebellion in Kabul and was for a long time preoccupied with frontier problems. He spent some years in the Punjab during which he annexed Kashmir (1580). Meanwhile his commanders took Sindh (1597) and principalities of the Deccan. Akbar sanctioned the conquest of the South. After a long sojourn in Kashmir ("my private garden") he personally supervised the annexation of Andhra. By 1600 his domains extended from Afghanistan to Bengal and from Kashmir down to the southern extremities of the Deccan plateau.

The title "Great" attached by historians to Akbar's name is not by virtue of his conquests but for his equitable administration and the humane treatment of his subjects. "If I were guilty of an unjust act," he once said, "I would rise in judgement against myself." He introduced reforms in the collection of revenue and put his civil services on a proper footing. He patronised the arts and raised many buildings. Above all, it was his concept of a secular state in which his subjects of diverse races and religious affiliations enjoyed equal rights that gave him a lasting place in history. His attempt to formulate an eclectic faith, combining what he considered to be the best in Islam, Zoroastrianism, Hinduism, Jainism and Christianity, with himself as the divine godhead, was also a move in the same direction. It was these ideals that evoked praise from Sleeman: "Akbar has always appeared to me among sovereigns what Shakespeare was among poets."

Akbar was fortunate in the many able men who advised him. There was Abdur Rahim Khan-i-Khanan, son of Akbar's guardian-tutor of the earlier days, Bairam Khan. He took Todar Mal who had done such an excellent job for Sher Shah Suri, and Birbal, another Hindu, who combined the wit of court-jester with an uncanny ability for accounting and administration. Akbar also had his coterie of sycophants. Leading amongst them was the talented family of scholar-philosophers, Shaikh Mubarak and his sons Abul Fazl and Faizi. But there were a few, like the historian Badauni, who hated Akbar's and his courtiers' trifling with Islam; he could, however, do little except turn his venomous quill to pen his thoughts in his private diary.

For administrative and revenue purposes, the country was divided into twelve *subas* (provinces) under a *subedar* (governor) with a coterie of officials below him. They were charged with matters of finance, the disbursement of salaries, police, justice, grants, excise, and record-keeping. The state's share of revenue was calculated for every year (about one-third of the gross yield in the north, half in the Deccan). An attempt at a ten-year settlement proved too harsh. The men behind these administrative measures were Todar Mal and Muzaffar Khan Turbatai.

Akbar reorganised his armed forces by reducing the standing army and relying more on the militias of nobility who were given grants of land. He created a complex system of *mansabdars* of 33 grades, ranging from the lowest (who were expected to provide 10 horsemen) to the highest (who were expected to provide 5,000). The administration of civil and military matters required a secretariat: Akbar had 1,600 civil servants on his permanent staff.

Akbar's father and grandfather did not have much time to patronise the arts. It was left to the illiterate Akbar to make amends. He collected a library of 24,000 manuscripts at an estimated cost of some 6.5 million rupees and engaged calligraphists known for their mastery of style. His favourite was the Kashmiri, Mohammed Hussain, on whom he bestowed the title *Zarrin-Kalam* ("Gold Pen").

Akbar surrounded himself with scholars, poets, theologians, painters and musicians. The top nine (which included some philistine ministers) came to be known as the "nine gems" (*nava ratna*). Chief of the cultural elite were Abul Fazl and his versifier brother, Faizi. Birbal was included by virtue of his gift of repartee (ripostes between Birbal and Mulla Do Piaza are to this day great favourites amongst the people). Then, there was the singer, Tansen, of Gwalior – still the greatest name in north Indian vocal music. Akbar ignored the Islamic injunction against portraying living things. "There are many that hate painting; but such men I dislike," said the aesthetic Emperor, alluding to the bigots. "It appears to me as if a painter had quite a peculiar means of recognising God." Of the seventeen court painters listed, thirteen were Hindus.

It was perhaps a historical coincidence that two of the greatest figures in Hindi religious poetry also flourished in Akbar's time. Tulsidas (1623) lived in Benares where he composed the monumental *Ram Charit Manas* ("Lake of Rama's Deeds") – still the most popular versified rendering of the great Hindu epic. The other was the blind hymn singer Surdas, whose father was employed at court.

Akbar was also a great builder. "His Majesty plans splendid edifices and dresses the works of his mind and heart in the garment of stone and clay," noted Abul Fazl. Unfortunately many of Akbar's buildings were demolished by his grandson Shah Jahan and the material used to construct others. Nevertheless, much remains: the mausoleum of his father in Delhi, considered by many to be the progenitor of the Taj; portions of the fort palaces in Agra; the red sandstone city of Fatehpur sikri with its massive *Buland Darwaza;* the tomb of the saint Salim Chishti and the palaces of his Hindu wife, Jodha Bai. All these bear testimony to the skill of the stoneworkers and the grand designs of Akbar's architects. In these monuments, Akbar's eclecticism – the Hindu style blended with the Muslim – is beautifully portrayed.

Akbar's dream of creating an Indian religion compounded of the various creeds practised in the country deserves attention. It was during a particularly bloody hunting expedition in 1578 at Bhera that Akbar was overcome by remorse and ordered, "No one should touch the feather of a finch ... allow all animals to depart according to their habits." (Abul Fazl.) He toyed with the idea of abdicating, of "entirely gathering up the skirt of his genius from earthly pomp". While resting under a tree, he had a mystic experience. "Take care!" warned Badauni, "the grace of God comes suddenly. It comes suddenly, it comes to the mind of the wise."

Akbar gave away gold to *fakirs*, shaved his head and returned to Agra determined to renounce kingship. He did not go ahead with the resolve but embarked on a study of different faiths. First he came under the influence of a Zoroastrian, Dastur Meherji Rana of Navsari. Akbar began to worship the light. "To light a candle is to commemorate the rising of the sun," he said and ordered that everyone should rise when lamps were lit. A hapless lamplighter who fell asleep and let the lamp burn out was executed.

Then he turned to Jainism. He heard Hari Vijay Suri and renounced eating meat. "I will not make my body a tomb for beasts," he said. Then came the turn of Christianity. He received a number of Jesuit missions, kissed their Bibles and other religious insignia – and took a Christian wife. He honoured the Sikh Guru, Amar Das, and heard recitation of Sikh hymns. Islam and Hinduism had always been with him and debates on religion had been going on in the hall of worship (*ibadat khana*) since 1575. "Discourses on philosophy have such a charm for me that they distract me from all else," he said. Sometimes he spent the whole night in prayer and meditated till the early hours, sitting on a large flat stone with his head bent over his chest. Out of these spiritual vats he (or rather his courtiers, Abul Fazl and Faizi) prepared a heady cocktail. *Din-i-Ilahi* ("The Faith of Allah") declared Akbar as the Viceregent of God on earth and therefore infallible. His name lent itself to the process of apotheosis. His followers greeted each other in the following manner: One said *Allah-o-Akbar* – God is Great (Akbar); the other replied: *Jalle-Jalal-hu* ("Glorious in His Glory"); Akbar's first name was Jalaluddin.

Not many people took Akbar's excursions into theology very seriously. "Religion and law are the concerns of prophets, not the business of kings," the Muslim *kotwal* of Delhi boldly reminded his monarch. Even his Rajput kinsman and friend, Man Singh, refused to acknowledge Akbar as his spiritual head. "I am willing to sacrifice my life for you ... I am a Hindu and am willing to be Muslim but know no other religion," he said. The only Hindu listed amongst his followers was the Brahmin upstart, Birbal.

It is more than likely that after some years of appearing as a human god, Akbar himself got tired of the posture. If Badauni is to be believed, even Abul Fazl confessed to him that he "wished to wander for a few days in the vale of infidelity". (Badauni hated Abul Fazl whom he described as "officious, time-serving, openly faithless, continuously studying the Emperor's whims, a flatterer beyond all bounds". Abul Fazl was given to the luxuries of life. "He was a prodigious eater and fornicator.")

Akbar realised the truth of the saying he earlier had inscribed in the *Buland Darwaza* at Sikri: "Said Jesus (on whom be peace) the world is a bridge; pass over it, but build no houses on it."

The importance of Akbar's experiment is the concept it generated, viz., Indians could perhaps be one nation with one faith.

Akbar's reign is also significant for the first real contact that India's ruler had with European powers, notably the Portuguese and the English. Akbar was disturbed by this intrusion. He is reported to have said: "I have kept before my mind the idea that I should undertake the destruction of the *ferringhee* infidels who have come to the islands of our ocean ... they have come in great numbers and are a stumbling block to the pilgrims and traders. We have thought of going in person and cleansing that road of thorns and weeds." But Akbar had no navy worth mentioning and had to make terms with the *ferringhees*. In 1603 John Mildenhall paid a courtesy call on the Emperor at Lahore and presented a letter from Queen Elizabeth. The Portuguese Jesuits were much put out by the arrival of "English thieves and spies". However, all that Akbar was able to get from the Europeans was an assurance that Haj pilgrims and India's sea-going trade would not be interfered with.

Akbar's last years were saddened by the rebellion of the heir-apparent, Jehangir. He kept the prince under house arrest for four years and even contemplated passing succession to a younger son. But death overtook him in the early hours of Thursday, 27 October 1605.

Jehangir (1605-27)

Jehangir was as different from his sire as any son could be from his father. He was erudite while his father had been illiterate; vicious where his father was magnanimous: and although born of a Hindu mother and married to a Hindu princess (who killed herself when shamed by her husband's revolt against his father) he had none of the visions of creating a state in which all subjects had equal rights. As a result, his many achievements are overlooked. He was able to keep his inheritance together by keeping down the Rajputs and by quelling the attempts of the Deccani Muslims to make themselves independent. Jehangir also made notable advances in the art of building: his father's mausoleum at Sikandara (seven miles north of Agra). The bejewelled *Itmad-ud-daulah* along the Jumna, where marble craftsmen showed superb skill in stone inlay work; the royal mosque at Lahore; the gardens in Lahore and the Vale of Kashmir – all these bear testimony to his vision of beauty. His coins and medallions were also vastly superior to those of his ancestors.

In the popular mind, Jehangir's twenty-two year reign is remembered for his carousing – prolonged bouts of drinking and dalliance, first with the legendary Anarkali, then with the beautiful Noor Jehan whom he acquired by contriving the murder of her husband. He also took a sadist's delight in ordering and watching executions: he forced his rebellious son, Khurram, to ride with him to witness his supporters' agonies while they were impaled on stakes or their bodies trampled over by elephants. However, he failed to keep down his ambitious, impatient progeny from revolting against his authority.

Shah Jahan (1627-66)

Shah Jahan, like his father, was thirty-five when he became king and, like his father, had to kill his brothers before he was able to secure the throne for himself. Fratricidal contests for the throne had by now become an established tradition of the house of the Mughals. As a result, the many principalities which had either sided with the loser or had made a bid for freedom had to be reconquered.

Shah Jahan had to spend sixteen of his thirty-two years as Emperor in campaigns against the irrepressible Rajputs and the Deccan kingdoms. He, too, despite a generous dose of Hindu blood in his veins, victimised his Hindu subjects by imposing the humiliating *jiziya* and even destroying their places of worship.

Shah Jahan's shortcomings as a monarch were obliterated by the magnificent buildings raised in his time: the palaces and the Pearl Mosque in the fort at Agra; the Royal Mosque – the biggest and the most beautiful of all mosques of the world – at Delhi; the Red Fort in Delhi; innumerable gardens in different parts of India; and above all the divinely conceived and executed Taj Mahal, raised to enshrine the dust of his favourite queen and mother of fourteen of his children. All these justify the title, "the greatest builder of all times".

Shah Jahan spent the last seven-and-a-half years of his life under house arrest ordered by his son, Aurangzeb. He died on 22 January 1666.

Aurangzeb (1666-1707)

Historians are sharply divided on their estimates of Aurangzeb. The controversy is not limited to books of history but is a live issue amongst the historians of Pakistan on one side and the Indians on the other. Aurangzeb ruled an empire bigger than Akbar's, and for as long a time. He was a puritan. He did not touch liquor. He disapproved of dancing and music. He inherited little of the amorous traits which had sullied the names of his forefathers. He was a devout Muslim who spent many hours of the day in prayer and in making copies of the Quran. He stitched caps to raise money for his shroud. He was always simply dressed and lived frugally. He was fearless ("That man alone can tightly clasp in his arms the bride of kingship who can kiss the keen sword's lip," he wrote). He was for ever putting down rebellions and extending his domains ("... a ruler should always be on the move ... being in one place gives impression of repose but brings a thousand calamities"). This was only one aspect of his character. He was also rapacious, calculating, ambitious and treacherous. He tricked and slew his brothers and their sons, kept his father in prison and reduced his non-Muslim subjects to the rank of second-class citizens. When they revolted against him, he put them down with a severity which evoked memories of the savage Turks and renewed the image of the Muslim as a bigot. This was the treatment meted out to the Jats of Mathura and Agra in 1669; to the Satnamis and Mundas at Narnaul in 1672; to the ninth Guru of the Sikhs, Tegh Bahadur, in 1675. He tried to do the same towards the Rajputs and the Marathas. He did not even spare the Shia Muslims (*ghul-i-bayabani* – "corpse-eating devils", as he described them) nor the peace-loving Sufis.

He was such a stickler for the letter of Islamic law that, despite his learning, he looked upon the arts and music as the inventions of Satan. Though descended from a long line of builders, all he left behind him were some mosques (a very beautiful one in the Red Fort of Delhi and another in Benares raised over the ruins of Hindu temples). Aurangzeb was veritably a Jekyll-Hyde character and people (including the historians) admired or loathed him according to which aspect they saw of him.

It was historical justice that the very people Aurangzeb sought to destroy, in turn destroyed the Mughal rule in India – the Jats, the Sikhs and, above all, the Marathas who rose under their great leader, Shivaji, and later reduced Aurangzeb's successors to the lowly status of pensioners.

The first to rise were the Jats of Mathura and Agra. Their leader, Gokla, held the Mughal army at bay at Tilpat (less than twenty miles from Delhi) for several days till he and 7,000 of his fellow Jats were slain (1669). Three years later the Satnamis rose at Narnaul and had to be put down with savage reprisals. In 1675, Tegh Bahadur, the ninth Guru of the Sikhs was executed in Delhi – and the seeds of a Sikh uprising were sown. The most powerful of all the Hindu resistance movements was launched by the Marathas. Shivaji, son of a Hindu chieftain in the employ of the Muslim ruler of Bijapur, roused the Mavli hillmen of the western coast of the Deccan and by a combination of daring, cunning and plain treachery acquired a number of forts in the Ghats. In 1659 he tricked and slew Afzal Khan and decimated the army sent against him from Bijapur. A year later he surprised the Mughal Emperor's uncle, Shahista Khan, who had expelled him from Poona and almost killed him (he chopped off three of his fingers). Four years later he plundered Surat. The Mughals sent a large army against him and forced him to sign away twenty-three of his forts (leaving him only twelve) and tricked him into visiting Delhi and then placing him under house arrest. Shivaji and his son escaped and returned to renew the capture of forts, the plundering of rich cities and the levying of *chauth* (a quarter of the total revenue as protection money). In June 1674, Shivaji had himself crowned King – *Chhatrapati* ("Bearer of the Royal Umbrella"). He died in 1680.

Although Aurangzeb was able to recover all the lands and forts captured by Shivaji – and executed Shivaji's son Sambhaji, the Marathas rose again under new commanders to replace the Mughals as rulers of India.

What were the major achievements of the Mughal rule? What were the chief causes of its downfall? These two are standard questions for all history examinations in Indian universities – and are answered by listing six or seven points.

Achievements: two hundred years of security from external invasion and internal disorder. Two hundred years that gave northern India political unity; closer contacts between Hindus and Muslims; development of the Urdu language and etiquette; development of painting, music, architecture and a sense of historiography; contact with European powers. And so on.

Causes of downfall: decadence of the monarchy and the nobility leading to the demoralisation of the army and the civil service; insufficient attention to agriculture and commerce leading to economic bankruptcy; religious intolerance of Shah Jahan and Aurangzeb leading to Hindu resistance movements of the Rajputs, Marathas, Jats and the Sikhs; indolence and parasitism of the privileged Muslims; weakening of the Central Government; wasteful campaigns in the Deccan and consequent inability to resist foreign invasions.

The Later Mughals

Aurangzeb's son, Bahadur Shah, had to spend much of his energy fighting his own brothers and then the Sikhs who had risen under Banda. He died broken-hearted and almost insane with frustration.

Thereafter, one Mughal followed another in quick succession – brother killed brother, uncle killed nephew, Some gave themselves to drink, others to common whores or indulged in heterosexual orgies. The most colourful of the debauchees was Mohammed Shah, aptly named *Rangeela*, "the Colourful One". His domain was confined to the city of Delhi. India was wide open to the invader.

A shattering blow was struck by the Persian invader, Nadir Shah. He entered India in 1739, defeated *Rangeela's* forces at Karnal and occupied Delhi. He stripped the capital of all its wealth. In one morning, Sunday the eleventh of March, he ordered a general massacre of the citizens and slew an estimated 15,000 men and women. In five months' stay in India he wrecked whatever was left of the administration, took enormous loot – including the fabulous Peacock Throne and the Koh-i-noor diamond. All he left was the Mughal king and an empty shell of what at one time had been the most powerful empire in Asia.

The final blow was struck by Nadir Shah's general, Ahmed Shah Abdali. In a series of nine invasions, Abdali completed the task of destruction. On the fifth invasion, he significantly defeated the Marathas (at Panipat, 14 January 1761), thus giving the Sikhs a chance to fill the vacuum in northern India. The Marathas, however, recovered from the blow. Thereafter, the contending powers in India were the Marathas, the Jats, the Sikhs and the English. The Mughal was only a nominal monarch. His territory, as the adage went, extended from Delhi to Palam – seven miles west of the capital:

"Saltnat Shah Alam
Az Dilli to Palam."

Macaulay compared India after the death of Aurangzeb with the wide dominion of the Franks after the death of Charlemagne who began to bring contempt on themselves and destruction on their subjects … In the forty years following the death of Aurangzeb "a succession of nominal sovereigns, sunk in indolence and debauchery, wasted away life in secluded palaces chewing *bhang*, fondling concubines, and listening to buffoons". A succession of previous invaders descended through the western passes to prey on the defenceless wealth of Hindustan … and every corner of the wide empire learned to tremble at the mighty name of the Marathas … wherever their kettle-drums were heard, the peasant threw his bag of rice on his shoulder, hid his small savings in his girdle, and fled with his wife and children to the mountains or jungles, to the milder neighbourhood of the hyena and the tiger.

13

British India

*E*uropeans had known about India long before they came to it. During the heyday of the cities of the Indus Valley, ships and caravans carried Indian products to Babylonia, Assyria and Mesopotamia and thence to Europe. It is not unlikely that stories of India's wealth induced tribes from the Caucasian regions to abandon their homes and turn to India. But it is to the Greeks under Alexander (326 BC) that the credit is often given for the European discovery of India. However, the Europeans were unable to exploit this discovery, as the Muslims came to control the land and sea routes and for almost 1,000 years excluded others from coming to India.

The Arab supremacy of the sea routes was challenged by the Portuguese. In 1486 Bartholomew

Diaz rounded the Cape of Good Hope. Twelve years later (1498) Vasco da Gama travelled the same route and dropped anchor at Calicut. He loaded his three ships with spices, silks, ivory and sandalwood and on his return to Lisbon sold the cargo for a profit that was sixty times more than the cost of the voyage. He returned with twenty ships and established a warehouse at Cochin. For the next hundred years, Portuguese merchant ships and men-of-war held the "gorgeous east in fee".

The Portuguese acquired Goa in 1510 and made it their headquarters. Their other warehouses were at Diu, Daman and Cochin. From the start they had designs of making India a Christian colony of the Portuguese empire. The Governor of Goa, Alphonso de Albuquerque (1509-15), converted his warehouses into fortresses and mingled trade with the acquisition of territory. He supported Catholic missions. Francis Xavier converted large sections of the coastal population in Goa to Catholicism. The Portuguese also encouraged their men to take Indian wives. Within a few decades the west coast had a mestizo population of Indo-Portuguese extraction speaking Marathi, Konkani and Portuguese.

The Portuguese were not able to retain their monopoly over the Arabian Sea and the Indian Ocean, nor expand into the hinterland of India. The Dutch successfully challenged their dominion over the waters; the Marathas kept them hemmed to the sea coast.

Their way of life – hard drinking and fornication combined with maltreatment of the native population – thwarted their design of creating a Portuguese Christian empire in the east. They abandoned India and diverted their energies to Brazil.

The Portuguese left a valuable legacy for India. They introduced new crops like maize, potatoes and tobacco. They gave Catholicism a powerful base in Goa. The Goans have preserved much of the Portuguese way of life and culture. European food, wine, music and dancing are to this day a speciality of the Goan Catholic.

The Dutch were the next to set up fortified trading ports in India. They started with sites near present-day Madras and then expanded towards the western coast and to Bengal. They were compelled to relinquish their Indian possessions to the English and found it more profitable to concentrate their energies on acquiring an empire in present-day Indonesia.

Equally brief was the sojourn of the Danes. In 1616 they acquired a foothold at Serampore in Bengal where they allowed Protestant missions to set up a printing press. They also found their Indian enterprise unprofitable, sold Serampore to the English, and finally withdrew from India in 1845.

The real contest for dominion in India was between the French and the English. Before we turn to the Anglo-French confrontation, it would be profitable to know what induced Europeans to venture out to Asian countries. Initially it was to buy goods produced in these (then the more advanced) countries in exchange for their own. There was a good market for Oriental spices and herbs which were in those days used to preserve meat. The Europeans had developed the art of warfare more than the peoples of the countries they came to trade with, and they soon found that carrying a musket on the shoulder produced a better bargain. They explored all countries of the Orient and for a while left China and Japan alone because they did not grow spices. It was India, Sri Lanka, Burma, Malaya and Indo-China which became the hunting ground of European merchants.

Although the French came later on the scene (it was at Colbert's initiative that a French East India Company was formed in 1669) they had the upper hand for more than 50 years. Under the able leadership of Dupleix, they expelled the British from Madras (later restored to them by the Treaty of Aix la Chapelle) and through arrangements with Indian rulers brought large parts of the Deccan under their control.

The Franco-British conflict in India was really an extension of the contest between the two in Europe during the war of the Austrian Succession (1740-48) and the Seven Years' War (1756-63).

English travellers, missionaries and tradesmen are known to have started coming to India in the latter part of the sixteenth century. After defeating the Spanish Armada in 1588, English ships began to venture further overseas. In 1600 the East India Company was granted a charter for exclusive trading rights with India for fifteen years. The earlier ventures were wildly successful: profits from the spice trade were augmented by plundering ships. By 1612 the English had ejected the Portuguese and the Dutch from Indian waters, acquired a trading post (known as a factory) at Surat, and the English ambassador, Sir Thomas Roe, a gentleman "of pregnant understanding and comely personage" was in attendance at the court of the Mughal Emperor, Jehangir. The "Dutch seek plantation by the sword," opined the sagacious diplomat-cum-trader. "Let this be received as a rule, that if you will profit, seek it at sea in quiet trade and without controversy; it is an error to effect garrisons and land wars in India." In the next couple of decades, the English established many more factories. Although the primary motive was trade, they garrisoned their factories and were not averse to using force in furtherance of profit. The twenty years between 1660 and 1680 yielded larger profits: they paid a dividend of 25 per cent to the Company's shareholders. Its employees in India lined their pockets with *sicca* rupees.

In 1639 the East India Company acquired Madras. In 1668 it got the island of Bombay for a rent of £10 per year, from its sovereign, Charles II (who had in his turn acquired it in the dowry of his Portuguese wife). It was this kind of grabbing and exploitation that inspired Adam Smith to describe the East India

Company as a body "for the apportionment of the plunder of India".

By the turn of the century, the English were firmly entrenched on the Indian coast stretching from Surat to Bombay in the west and from Madras to Calcutta in the east. They were strong enough to seize ships of the most powerful of all Mughal emperors, Aurangzeb. Thereafter, as the Mughal Empire began to disintegrate, their only serious rivals were the French and the Marathas.

The English triumph over the French was due to English commercial and military superiority. The English made their Indian conquests pay; the French did not. Consequently, while the English Company enjoyed a measure of independence to make alliances with native rulers and to recruit native mercenaries to fight for them, the French Company remained a creature of the Government in Paris and the military reverse of France in Europe had an adverse effect on the *Campagnie* in India. The English were also lucky in their choice of commanders. Men like Robert Clive and Stringer Lawrence were gifted soldiers. In a few years the English navy came to rule the Indian seas and the English army became the most powerful in Hindustan.

As soon as the rival European powers were disposed of, the English began to extend their dominion over India.

The first blow was struck in Bengal. In the summer of 1756 the young Nawab Siraj-ud-Dowlah (known to be a Francophile), after much needling, captured a party of English men and women and clapped them in gaol. Exact details of what transpired are disputed between Indian and British historians. The English assert that of the 146 people who were locked up in a cell, 123 died of heat and suffocation. The English made full use of this "Black Hole" tragedy to wreak vengeance on the Nawab. Robert Clive, leading an army of a few hundred white soldiers and a few thousand natives, signally defeated the Nawab's 60,000-strong army on the battlefield of Plassey – and so acquired Bengal for England. Clive was rewarded by being made governor of the provinces. He turned the post to one of great profit, amassing a large fortune for himself. Seven years later, Clive needled the Nawab he had installed in the place of Siraj-ud-Dowlah into rebellion, defeated him and took large areas of Bihar and Orissa. Clive got a second term as governor and made a second fortune. The Mughal Emperor was persuaded, by token payments, to confirm these acquisitions for seven years; and when the seven years were over (1771), John Company simply assumed sovereignty. It set up a Board of Control to administer the territories acquired.

Clive returned home loaded with money. Envious tongues made accusations of corruption on a nabobic scale. Clive's conscience drove him to take his own life.

Meanwhile in India the English continued to add to their territories around Madras. They made and unmade alliances with the Marathas; first compensated them for the help they had given against the French – and then taking it all back in 1782 to punish them for their truculence. Territories of some native rulers were annexed outright; others discreetly acknowledged Britain as the paramount power and signed treaties which guaranteed them a measure of autonomy and the continuance of their dynasties. Yet some others were conquered and turned over to subservient nobility. Thus after victorious campaigns against Hyder Ali and his son Tippu (1767-69, 1780-84 and 1790-92), the Muslim ruling family was eliminated and a Hindu installed as the Raja of Mysore. The Maratha confederacies were reduced piecemeal between 1775-82, 1803-05 and 1817-19. By eliminating the Marathas and the Jats, the English became the overlords of Delhi

Tippu Sultan

(1801) and the adjacent territories. The Mughal Emperor who had been a pensioner of the Marathas became the pensioner of the English.

Burma was taken in two campaigns in 1824-26 and 1852. The Nepalese were defeated (1814-16) but allowed to continue to run their mountainous kingdom; the Afghans were humbled in 1839-42. Sindh was conquered and annexed. The last remaining independent Indian power, the Sikhs, were provoked into a war in 1845-46, defeated, and made to part with half their kingdom. Two years later after another war, the rest of the Sikh kingdom was also annexed (1849). The young Sikh Maharajah was made to hand over the Koh-i-noor diamond (which his father Ranjit Singh had extracted from the Afghans), and sent to England to spend his remaining years in pensioned extravagance.

During these years of conquest and consolidation, John Company underwent many changes in its constitution and functions. By a Regulating Act passed in 1773, the British Parliament appointed a governor-general in Calcutta, took over the political functions in its own hands and imposed a time limit on the Company's trading monopoly in India. The political take-over was confirmed by the second Regulating Act passed in 1774. In 1813, the Company's monopoly over trade was ended.

One concerted effort made by the Indians to rid themselves of the foreign yoke took place in the summer of 1857. Once again, English and Indian historians are at variance regarding the causes, extent and nature of the uprising. The English describe it as a mutiny of native mercenaries, exploited by a few disgruntled princelings who had been divested of power. Most Indians describe it as the first war of Indian independence. It was a mixture of both. Not all Indians joined the revolt – and those that did had little identity of purpose save the desire to drive out the English and recover their kingdoms. After eighteen months of bitter fighting and savage reprisals the revolt was suppressed. The Mughal Emperor was exiled to Burma, John Company was wound up and India became a domain of the English sovereign.

★

How did the English come to acquire so vast a dominion with such ease? Why did the Indians put up so miserable a performance in resisting foreign encroachment?

Indians had never been a nation: they had been divided by religion, race, caste and language; the vast mass of the people were indifferent and frequently hostile to the princes and the nobility who monopolised leadership. The princes, owing loyalty only to themselves, were often more eager to see the downfall of their rivals than in forwarding their own interests; they were easily outmanoeuvred and outgunned by the better trained, better disciplined and better equipped soldiers of the Company. The English conquered India with the help of the Indians: Madrasi militia against the Marathas, Bengalis and Biharis against the Sikhs, Sikhs and Punjabi Muslims against the rest.

Indian disunity and military ineptitude were not the only factors; the readiness of so many Indians to serve the English rather than native rulers also accounted for the consolidation of the English empire. Without Indian collaborators, so small a body of foreigners could not have administered so vast a country inhabited by so diverse a people. It is in the dispassionate examination of the pros and cons of British rule in India that we find answers to the two questions: how did Britain come by so large an empire so easily and in so short a time? And how did so powerful an empire later crumble like a sandcastle before the tidal wave of Indian renaissance?

For the first time in its long history, India came to be administered by one government. Neither the Mauryas nor the Guptas, nor the Khiljis nor the Mughals had ruled the entire geographical extent of the subcontinent. No native ruler had administered his domains as effectively as did the British. Indian monarchs were constantly engaged in campaigns against recalcitrant governors and upstart dynasties: reconquest and not administration was given top priority. There were no such revolts against British domination. The only exception to the general rule of the sovereign government in the centre was the semi-autonomous status accorded to the 500-odd princely states. The effect of this unitary rule was to create a nascent sense of unity between the peoples of India and give birth to the feeling of Indianness. Hindu, yes; Muslim, yes; Christian or Sikh, yes – but also Indian. Bengali, Tamilian, Andhra and Punjabi, yes – but also Indian. For the first time Indians became conscious of a common destiny.

For the first time in thousands of years, Indians were rid of the spectre of foreign invasions. The British effectively sealed off the mountain passes through which conquerors had entered. And since they were masters of the seas no maritime power could venture into Indian waters. (The one instance of a breakthrough – it would be more accurate to describe it as a pin-prick – was in World War II when for a very brief period the Japanese-sponsored Indian National Army occupied the Andaman Islands and a tiny portion of Assam.)

The British enforcement of law and justice, though at times biased in cases of conflict between whites and Indians, dealt with all Indians as equals. Customary laws of different communities regulating inheritance, marriage, divorce, adoption, etc. were respected. The penal code, laws of contracts, torts and rules of evidence were uniformly applied to all citizens. No longer was justice dependent on the whims of the ruler; no discrimination was practised in favour of a Muslim against a Hindu, in favour of a Brahmin against an untouchable. Although legal procedures were complicated, expensive, corruptible – hence weighed heavily in favour of the rich and the powerful – they were standardised and, in honest hands, instruments of impartial justice.

The rule of law engendered the concept of civil liberty. No one could be detained without trial, apprehended without a warrant of arrest.

Not only did the British not discriminate against people on the grounds of race or religion, they strictly refrained from extending official patronage to Christian missions or from showing favours to Christian converts. This was markedly different from the attitude of Indian rulers towards men of their own religion or of the Europeans who preceded them.

British expansion in India coincided with the technological advances in the West which were, in due course, introduced into India. Steamships began to ply the Indian rivers. Commerce and defence requirements stimulated extension of the means of communication: 70,000 miles of metalled roads; 40,000 miles of rail track; telegraph and postal services; all were built by British enterprise. Critics pointed out that Britain gained more than India. All the capital equipment, technicians, personnel (except at the lowest level) came from Britain – which is where the profit went.

It was also the time when Britain wanted India to produce raw material for British factories: cotton and indigo were at a premium. A vast network of irrigation canals opened up 32 million acres of desert land in the Punjab which became India's granary and one of the major suppliers of cotton and indigo. Crops which yielded even bigger profits remained largely in British hands: tea and coffee estates were owned by English planters; though jute was grown by Indian peasants, jute mills were owned by the British.

Economists are not agreed on the balance of benefits derived from these measures. While the British point to the rapid increase in Indian produce (from £8 million worth in 1834 to £190 million in 1928), Indians argue that indigenous industries, like the manufacture of textiles, were forced to close down and India was turned to producing raw materials – jute, cotton, indigo, pulses wheat, oilseeds, hides, mineral ores. In fairness to the British, it must be admitted that Indian industry also made advances. In 1890 there were only 700 registered factories; by 1939 the figure had risen to over 10,000, employing a labour force of two million men. The Tata steel works in Jamshedpur were the biggest in the British Empire.

The British introduced modern medicine, sanitation and health services. Malaria, cholera, smallpox and plague were controlled by mass inoculations. The figures of infant mortality came down; the population began to increase at an unprecedented rate. In some ways it was like clamping the lid on Pandora's box of epidemics and then reopening it to release a vast mass of humanity which the land could not feed, clothe, house or educate.

No Indian can deny British influence in bringing about social reforms in Indian society. *Sati* and female infanticide were outlawed, *Thuggee* and slavery liquidated, progressive elements were encouraged to raise the age of marriage and allow widows to remarry.

England gave India a good, stable and efficient government. "Efficiency," said the Viceroy, Lord Curzon (1899-1905), "has been our gospel, the keynote of our administration." Indians had not known administrators more competent and less corruptible than the English members of the Indian Civil Service. Although by 1883 the Service began to admit Indians, their number was very small and advancement extremely restricted. By 1864 there was only one Indian in the ICS; three in 1871; up to World War I, 80 per cent of the ICS was still English. It was not solely out of consideration towards the subject peoples that the English ruled with a fair but iron hand. Lord Lawrence, the Viceroy, said quite bluntly: "In doing the best we can for the people, we are bound by our conscience and not by theirs." The same Lawrence who had earlier told the Punjabis, "I will rule you with pen or sword," later in 1858 said to the Indians: "We have not been elected or placed in power by the people, but we are here through our moral superiority, by the force of circumstances, by the will of Providence. This alone constitutes our charter to govern India."

The cultural contact between the two peoples benefited India more than the British. British Indologists made Indians conscious of their heritage in art, architecture and literature. They translated Sanskrit classics (rediscovering the Gita for the Hindus) and preserved their monuments and caves. Some names deserve mention. Sir William Jones (1746-94), the Calcutta judge who translated Kalidas's *Shakuntala* and drew attention to the kinship between Greek, Latin and Sanskrit; Sir Charles Wilkins (1749-1836), translator of the Gita (in 1780) and the *Hitopadesha*, William Robertson (1721-93), who collaborated with Sir William Jones; and many others, like William Wilkins, Horace Wilson and Colebrooke.

The English also introduced their language into India. This was done after much debate on whether it was best to continue the use of different regional languages, with Persian as the official *lingua franca*, or replace them by English. The issue was settled in 1835 by Macaulay who had very little respect for Oriental scholarship. "One shelf of a library in Europe is worth all the learning of the East," he wrote. Accordingly, English replaced Persian in offices and law courts and came to be taught as a compulsory subject in high schools and colleges. This was a mixed blessing. White English gave Indians speaking different languages a common language of communication, it remained confined to the upper elite: never did more than two per cent of the population learn to speak it. This added to the existing disparity between the privileged and the unprivileged masses. By learning English the privileged gained access to the learning of the West – its sciences, philosophy, its political concepts like equality, freedom and democracy. English gave the affluent classes a monopoly of leadership and kept the poor masses in political sub-service for a century or more.

It is a strange phenomenon that although many Indians came to know the English language uncommonly well – perhaps better than any other people who did not have it as their mother tongue – they made very little contribution to its literature. Those who studied it did so largely to enhance their prospects in life. Hence, though English took in a large number of words from Indian languages (the dictionary Hobson-Jobson lists over 3,000 words of Indian origin in the English lexicon), Indians, as soon as they were free, got about replacing English words by coining new ones of their own.

India produced a number of distinguished English novelists and poets like Flora Annie Steele, Thackeray, Rudyard Kipling, Myers, Edward Thompson, E.M. Forster, John Masters and the Durrels (Lawrence and Gerald). Many others who never came to India were nevertheless inspired by her: Goethe, Emerson, Tolstoy, Thoreau, Hermann Hesse.

The English language brought in notions of freedom and in turn compelled the English to put their professions into practice. In slow stages, they introduced parliamentary institutions in the country. At first the franchise was restricted to the propertied and the educated classes and very little responsibility given to elected councils. But as pressure from the English-educated Indians developed, the franchise was widened and more power was passed to Indian hands. This process can be discerned in the succession of Indian Councils Acts, the Morley-Minto reforms (1909), the Montagu-Chelmsford reforms (1919) and the

Government of India Act of 1935. English was the language of India's freedom movement.

There is little doubt that England ruled India by the willing cooperation of the majority of Indians. At the turn of the century, out of a total of some 500,000 civil servants of all grades, only about 4,000 were English. As late as 1931 there were only 168,000 Englishmen in India, of whom 80,000 were in the army, 21,000 in business or the professions, and 12,000 with the civil service. There was never more than one Englishman to every 4,000 Indians. The British were able to rule by keeping key positions in their own hands and by the consent of the people they ruled.

The Indian nationalist does not accept this interpretation of Indo-British history. Romesh Dutt (1848-1909), author, lecturer and one-time President of the Indian National Congress, said, "History does not record a single instance of one people ruling another in the interests of the subject nation." So, said Dutt, it was with the English in India. England, its trade and commerce, its defence requirements and its people came first; India's needs and Indians came a poor second.

England reduced India to beggary, say most Indian nationalists. Till the eighteenth century India was a producer nation. Her textiles were in great demand in Europe and her agricultural produce was enough to feed her population, with a surplus to sell abroad.

Only a little more than half the population got their living from the land. The English allowed that state of affairs to continue as long as it suited them. The Industrial Revolution changed everything. England began to produce finished goods and wanted markets for them. With a concerted effort the English ruined India's textile industry, put millions of weavers out of work, forced farmers to switch to raising cash crops needed for the British machines and thus played havoc with India's agricultural pattern. Figures bear out this criticism. When India was the exporter and Britain the importer, John Company had got special authorisation to take £130,000 worth of silver and gold to pay for its Indian purchases. When the roles were reversed, India became England's debtor. Its sterling debt mounted with the years. Britain virtually excluded the rest of the world from the Indian market. While the English dumped their textiles on India, they taxed Indian textiles destined for England. In later years when the English discovered that there were other ways of making money in India, they established tea and coffee plantations and jute and textile mills. By their own reckoning, by 1929, British capital in India was between £573 and £700 million. In 1933 the British Associated Chambers of Commerce estimated British interests at £1,000 million, made up of a £379 million sterling debt, £500 million for British companies and other investments. One-fourth of all that the English owned outside Britain was in India.

The first people to be impoverished were the weavers. Their looms were idle; they had neither land nor any other skills to turn to. Thus millions became farm hands in a country which had little land to spare and already had a surplus of agricultural labourers. A combination of other factors initiated by the British administration resulted in an upheaval in the life of the agriculturist. These included: a higher rate of revenue payable in cash rather than in kind and enforced by attachment of holdings, and the compulsory switching from food grains to cash crops. For the farmer the choice was between lifelong servitude to the moneylender and starvation – or both. It is estimated that four famines (1877-78, 1892, 1897, 1900) took a total toll of 15 million lives. Famines had been known in India before and famine conditions have prevailed in India after the British left. The only difference was that during British times they were brought about by the callous indifference of the rulers.

Although the British administered India efficiently, they did so at an enormous cost to the Indian exchequer. The British civilian and army officers often drew salaries ten times those of their Indian counterparts. At one time (1901) half of the net revenues of India (£44 million) went towards payment for these services. It was the same in the development of communications. All purchases made in England were on a lavish scale. The first 6,000 miles of railway completed in 1872 cost India £100 million, which works out to over

£16,000 per mile. The story was repeated in other spheres: all the equipment for the army was of British manufacture and not till World War II was India allowed to start small arms manufacture of her own.

Britain created a class of people whose interests were closely tied to the continuance of British rule. The three most important were the princes, the so-called martial classes, and the brown bureaucracy. The princes were encouraged to retain a subordinate but separate identity; they were encouraged to remain irresponsible and autocratic to suppress democratic movements. In the defence services, the favoured mercenaries were the Gurkhas, Punjabi Mussalmans and the Sikhs. Although the ratio of British to Indian soldiers changed (roughly two British to five Indians), in the more strategic branches like heavy artillery, the ratio of Britons was much higher. Moreover, great care was taken to see that Indian soldiers never ganged up against them. The Punjab Committee on Reorganization, which, following the Great Mutiny, established the communal pattern of the Indian army, stated that "next to the grand counterpoise of a sufficient European force, comes the counterpoise of natives against natives." Indian soldiery were "neatly grouped into battalions, companies – and sometimes even platoons of specified classes".

Mr Nehru, somewhat bitterly, referred to the princes, "martial races" and the Brown Sahibs as "Quisling classes which were afraid of change". He described it as the "natural alliance" of British power with Indian reactionaries and held it responsible for many evil customs and practices by laws perpetuating the backwardness of women.

Indian critics maintain that the imposition of Western culture retarded the development of vernacular literature and the renaissance of Indian art, music and dancing. Mr Nehru was of the opinion that most of India's problems stemmed from "arrested growth". He said, "Indian civilisation went to seed because it became static, self-absorbed and inclined to narcissism." Notions of freedom, equality and justice that were lauded in English text books were rarely applied in India. For many years Indians were not encouraged to own printing presses. When Indian newspapers and journals eventually came out, they were published under severe restrictions. There never was any real freedom of the press under the British Raj.

The same, say the Indian nationalists, applied to democratic institutions. Britain held out against giving Indians more powers till the pressure of public opinion forced it to yield. Passive resistance movements and violent revolutionary activity always preceded commissions of enquiry and political concessions. And much as Britons may boast of their benign rule, there are many black pages in their Indian record: the vengeful attitude following the Mutiny, the Amritsar massacre (1919), the tyranny of martial law and the trials and tortures inflicted on hundreds of thousands of India's freedom fighters. There were also instances of racial arrogance: exclusive white clubs with notices reading, "No dogs or Indians allowed", apartheid in trains ("For Europeans and Anglo-Indians only"); the *nigger-gora* (honkey) syndrome that bedevilled social contact between the non-racist cultured Englishmen and cultured Indians.

Though the English gave India its unity, they were also responsible for its disunity and ultimate break-up into India and Pakistan. They played the divide-and-rule game with little subtlety. For some decades after the Mutiny, the Mussalman was the villain, the Hindu the pampered subject. After the Indian National Congress began to gather support, the Hindu became suspect, the Muslim was granted special privileges and encouraged to oppose the Hindu. The Muslim League (born 1906) was an egg hatched by Lord Minto's white leghorn. The most blatant example of the British design to alienate the Muslims from the Hindus was the partition of Bengal in order, as the *Statesman* of Calcutta – the leading organ of British opinion in India – wrote , "to foster in eastern Bengal the growth of a Mohammedan power, which, it is hoped, will have the effect of keeping in check the rapidly growing strength of the educated Hindu community." The governor of the new province publicly admitted the nature of the policy that was being pursued when he declared that he had two wives, one Hindu and one Moslem, but the Moslem wife was his favourite

(K.S. Shelvankar: *The Problem of India*, Penguin). The Muslims were given extra feed: separate electorates with weightage – and prodded on to cluck for more at the expense of the Hindus. The British did not create differences between Hindus and Muslims, but they exploited them as no rulers of India before them had done. The truth was succinctly put by Maulana Mohammed Ali, a nationalist Muslim: "It is the old maxim of divide and rule," he said. "But there is a division of labour here. We divide and you rule."

14

Freedom Movement-1

*T*he desire to get rid of foreigners must have been kindled in the hearts of some Indians almost as soon as the foreigners became rulers of the different parts of the country. Out of this xenophobia was born the xenophobic organisation of different persuasions.

The rising of 1857 is often described as India's first war of independence. But associations of Indians working for freedom were in existence before 1857. At the same time there were many others who openly disavowed the rising as mutiny and treachery and actively assisted the British to reassert their dominion over the country. Instead of trying to fix dates and discover the names of people who first protested against British rule, it would be more profitable to examine the class of leadership and the economic factors which gave rise to political agitation.

In India, leadership had been the monopoly of the landed aristocracy. The British conquered Indian by playing off one prince against another and extending their patronage to the most pliant and subservient. But the landed aristocracy, though maintained in power, was shorn of much of its traditional responsibilities and, consequently, alienated from the masses and rendered incapable of effective leadership. Meanwhile, British-sponsored schools and colleges began to turn out an increasingly larger number of Indians drawn from the middle classes. They became civil servants, journalists, lawyers, doctors and engineers. Since they had closer contacts with the people, they became moulders of public opinion and leaders of popular movements.

It is also noteworthy that regions first occupied by the British were also the first to revolt against their presence. It was in Maharashtra on the west coast and in Bengal in the east that the Indian freedom movements began before they spread to the Punjab and the rest of the country.

A factor which had a decisive bearing on the pattern of the freedom movements was the influence of religion. Since the vast majority of Indians were Hindus, it was to be expected that political movements would become involved in the renaissance of Hinduism. And since Hinduism meant many different things to different Hindus, they had different ideas on the role of non-Hindus and the shape they meant to give to the India of their dreams. There were some who conceived of India as essentially a Hindu state. Most voluble among them were the Arya Samajists who exhorted a return to the Vedas and advocated re-

Vivekananda

conversion of Muslims and Christians to Hinduism. The Brahmo-Samajists and the Theosophists, on the other hand, sought to evolve an eclectic faith compounded of Hinduism, Christianity and Sufistic Islam which would be acceptable to all Indians. There were also men like Ramakrishna and Vivekananda who, though ardent Hindus themselves, were eager to take people of other religious persuasions in the embrace of friendship. And there grew yet another class of young Hindus, often agnostic, who stubbornly refused to concede any role to religion in political matters.

The Muslims of India evolved corresponding attitudes towards the freedom movements and the non-Muslims. Although all Muslims eulogised the past glories of Muslim rule, some like the Wahabis ascribed its eclipse to the abandonment of the spartan traditions of pristine Islam. The Wahabis' cry was "Back to the Quran and the Hadith", and the holy war against the infidel – both English and Hindu. Slightly less fanatic were the Pan-Islamicists who regarded Muslims of other nations closer of kin than their fellow Indians who were not Muslims. They aimed at a *Pax Islamica* under a Muslim caliph. They were willing to make common cause with the Hindu if it served the cause of the caliphate.

A third, more pragmatic group regarded themselves, as indeed they were, Muslims in a non-Muslim country. They were eager to westernize themselves and collaborate with the British, provided they were assured that they would be able to maintain their distinct and separate identity as Muslims of India.

Finally, there was a fourth group who believed that the future of Indian Muslims lay in unqualified cooperation with other Indians. Such collaboration, they felt, would in no way impair their religious identity.

It is in the interaction of these complex attitudes of the Hindu and Muslim groups towards each other that the history of the Indian freedom movement should be scrutinised.

★

We shall bypass the early attempts (the British India Association founded in 1851, which pleaded for Indian participation in the administration and Surendra Nath Banerjee's Indian Association of 1876) and start with 1885, the conventionally accepted date for the beginning of the freedom movement. it was in this year that the Indian National Congress was formed.

Educated Indians were taken aback by the European agitation over the draft of the Ilbert Bill (1883), which extended the power to try Europeans to Indian magistrates. The Government gave in to the pressure exerted by white racist organisations and amended the legislation. At this time Indian sepoys were being used in conquest of Burma and the British press was discussing the possibility of employing Indian troops and money in a war to curtail Russian expansion in Asia. To meet the increased expense on the army, the Government reintroduced income tax (1886), increased duty on salt from Rs 2 to Rs 2.50 per maund and, while abolishing excise on British yarn and textiles entering India, levied duty on Indian textiles exported to England. All these grievances needed to be ventilated. In 1885 the Indian National Congress held its first session in Poona at which 142 Indian and English delegates participated. The moving spirits behind the organisation were retired civilians, Sir William Wedderburn and Allan Octavian Hume, who became its first President.

This first session debated taxes, military expenditure and the desirability of conducting the Indian Civil Service examination in India, as well as in London, so that Indians could compete for it.

For the first thirty years of its existence, the Indian National Congress remained a debating body. By 1909 its membership had risen to nearly 14,000 of which over 12,000 were Hindus (almost half being Brahmins), about 900 Muslims, 200 Parsis and 100 Christians. More than one-third of the members were lawyers, the remaining two-thirds being agriculturists or businessmen.

Shortly before the turn of the century, radical elements entered the organisation and the Congress membership was split into moderates and extremists. It was these radical elements that compelled many Muslims to leave the Congress and set up a political organisation of their own.

The most outstanding figure among the Congress radicals was Bal Gangadhar Tilak (1858-1920), a Chitpavan Brahmin lawyer turned journalist. At first Tilak was more interested in education than either law, journalism or politics. He started the New English School and organised the Deccan Education Society. Then he turned to journalism. In 1881 he began publishing two weekly journals, *Kesari* (Lion) in his native Marathi and the *Maratha* in English.

His religious and social views were those of orthodox Brahmins, verging on the obscurantist. In 1891 he opposed the Age of Consent Bill aimed at raising the age of marriage of girls from ten to twelve. At the same time, he tried to persuade the Congress to adopt cow-protection as a part of its programme. In order to make Maharashtrians more aware of their culture, Tilak revived in 1893 the ten-day annual celebration in honour of the elephant-headed God,

Ganesh or Ganapati, who always receives precedence over other gods in worship. Thus when a child starts his education, he is made to write *Shri Ganeshaya namah* ("I bow to Lord Ganesh"). Similarly, Ganesh is invoked for his blessing before entering a newly-built house by performing the *Gana-homa*, a sort of housewarming ceremony. During the Peshwa regime, there was public worship of this deity all over Maharashtra. The tenth and last day of the celebrations was – and still is – called *Anant-Chaturdashi*. This served to keep memories of *swaraj* alive in the minds of the people and also to remind them of their duty to work unitedly to regain the country's lost freedom by sinking their differences. With the same objective, Tilak also launched the observance of *Shivjayanti*, the celebration of the birth anniversary of Shivaji, the founder of the Maratha Empire. In fact, the Government of the day sanctioned an annual grant of Rs 5 towards the maintenance of Shivaji's *samadhi* (mausoleum) at Raigadh in Kolaba district in Maharashtra. Tilak-opposed the Epidemic Disease Bill, authorising compulsory inoculation against smallpox which had broken out in epidemic form in 1898, on the ground that it was an invasion of the privacy of Hindu homes.

Tilak's hero was the Maratha warrior, Shivaji, who had successfully defied the Mughals but whose name was anathema to the Muslims. Shivaji's birth anniversary began to be celebrated on a grand scale. In short, Tilak was an ardent Hindu nationalist who did not take Muslim loyalties for granted. He became a dominant figure in the Indian National Congress. It was not surprising that Muslims began to shy away from its sessions and in 1894 the Central Mohammedan Association passed a resolution "to hold aloof from Congress".

Tilak advocated the use of force to gain political ends. The first political murders of Europeans were perpetrated by his followers. In June 1897 the Chapekar brothers murdered a kindly British magistrate, Mr Rand, who was in charge of operations to combat smallpox. Tilak was given a charge-sheet for sedition.

Tilak's chief rival in the struggle for leadership was another Chitpavan Brahmin, Gopal Krishna Gokhale (1860-1915). Gokhale's Servants of India Society (1905) did commendable social service. By its constitution it "frankly accepted the British connection, as ordained in the inscrutable dispensation of Providence for India's good".

A similar brand of Hindu orientation was given to the Congress by new leaders in Bengal and the Punjab.

The radical movement in Bengal was triggered off by the proposal to partition the province. At that time Bengal included the provinces of Bihar and Orissa, which together had a population of 80 million. It was unwieldy, the people spoke different languages, and it had a heavy preponderance of Hindus. The Viceroy, Lord Curzon, planned to cut off the eastern districts (present-day Bangladesh) to create a new province where the Muslims would be in a majority. Curzon's motives were not altruistic. Under the pretext of better administration he wanted to segregate the Muslims of East Bengal, who were loyal to the British, from the Hindus of West Bengal who were not. He admitted that he would thus invest the Muslims of East Bengal with "a unity which they had not enjoyed since the days of the old Mughal Viceroys and Kings". Most Bengali Muslims welcomed the move. Most Bengali Hindus opposed it on the ground that the Bengalis were united in language, culture and race. Since the Bengali Hindus were better organised, more educated and more vocal, they made their resentment known in no uncertain manner. Their call for the boycott of British goods and the use of *swadeshi* brought the sales of English textiles during the autumn *Puja*-festival down by Rs 50 lakh. A national volunteer corps, the first of its kind, paraded the streets of Bengal cities. A secret terrorist organisation, sworn to murder Europeans and Indian loyalists and known as Anusilan Samiti, sprang up alongside peaceful agitation. It was significant that just as in Maharashtra, so also in Bengal the xenophobia drew its inspiration from Hinduism. In Maharashtra it was the revival of the cult of Ganapati and Shivaji; in Bengal it was through the revival of the cult of Kali, Shakti or Durga – the reincarnations of the goddess of destruction symbolised as Mother India. The goddess-mother thirsted for the blood of her white violators; it was up to her Indian (Hindu) sons to preserve her honour.

The upsurge of patriotism in Bengal was accompanied by the emergence of many writers and poets who also drew their inspiration from traditional Hinduism. Bankim Chandra Chatterji's novel *Anand Math* (1882) was based on the Sanyasi Rebellion of 1774 and included a hymn, *Bande Mataram* ("Salutations to the Motherland").

Rabindranath Tagore

The poet, Rabindranath Tagore, sang it at a session of the Indian National Congress in 1896 and it became the unofficial national anthem of India. A new prophet of Bengali Hindu nationalism, Sri Aurobindo, appeared on the scene. Sri Aurobindo, although he was educated in England, turned to Hinduism for guidance. After coming home in 1893 he began to publish a journal, *Indra Prakash*, which preached "purification by blood and fire". His pamphlet, *Bhawani Mandir* ("the Temple of Goddess Bhawani", who is also an incarnation of the goddess of destruction), was inspired by Bankim Chandra Chatterji's novel. Sri Aurobindo organised secret societies and extolled the use of the pistol and the bomb.

There was an outburst of terrorism in Bengal. Virtually all terrorists were Hindus. It was not very difficult for the English rulers to persuade the Muslims to keep away from an agitation led by idolatrous worshippers of Kali. While Bengali Hindus organised a day of "national" mourning (16 October 1905) to protest against the partition of their province, Nawab Salimullah of Dacca set up the Mohammedan Provincial Union to support the partition.

The pattern set by Maharashtra and Bengal was followed in the Punjab, except that for a while the agitators were successful in extending their operations from the cities to the countryside and also in bringing agricultural communities, including Muslims, under their influence. But even in the Punjab, Hindu Congress leaders mixed Hinduism with Nationalism and dampened the patriotic fervour of the Muslims.

In the Punjab the freedom movement was led by Lala Lajpat Rai, honoured by the title *Punjab Kesari* ("Lion of the Punjab"). Lajpat Rai was as ardent a nationalist as he was a supporter of Hindu revivalism. Many prominent members of the Punjab Congress were also members of the Arya Samaj, pledged to restoring Vedic purity to Hinduism, to the protection of cows and the reconversion of Muslims to Hinduism. Muslims could not forget that Dayanand Saraswati, the founder of the Arya Samaj, had in his *Satyarth Prakash*, made many uncomplimentary references to their Prophet.

In 1907, an agitation was organised in the Punjab against the Colonisation Bill. The leaders of the agitation were Lajpat Rai and Ajit Singh (another Sikhcum-Arya Samajist leader). For a while they succeeded in gaining support in the cities as well as in the new canal-irrigated colonies. But after their deportation, the freedom movement in the Punjab, as in Maharashtra and Bengal, developed into a movement of Hindu revivalism in which few Muslims agreed to participate. This was particularly noticeable in the Punjab terrorist organisations which drew their personnel almost exclusively from the ranks of the Arya Samaj.

The agitation in Bengal and the Punjab succeeded in attaining its object: the partition of Bengal was revoked in 1911 and the Punjab Colonisation Bill was withdrawn. But the price paid in terms of national solidarity was heavy. Indian Muslims began to turn their backs on the Hindu-oriented freedom movement. From 1905 onwards the number of Muslims attending the sessions of the Indian National Congress declined. They began to think in terms of organisations of their own. The ideas of Sir Syed Ahmed Khan, on the need to preserve Muslim separateness regained popularity. In 1906, the Muslim League was born.

Meanwhile, moderates in the Congress (Sir Phirozeshah Mehta, Dadabhai Naoroji and Gokhale) began to be edged out of power and radicals like Lala Lajpat Rai, Bal Gangadhar Tilak and the Bengali, Bipin Chandra Pal – the trio popularly described as "Lal, Bal and Pal" – came to the fore. Tilak castigated the moderates: "The three P's – pray, please, petition – are not enough," he said. B.C. Pal was equally forthright:

"We have been brought up for too long a period on constitutional reforms."

What made the radicals impatient was exposure to revolutionary ideas gaining popularity elsewhere in the world. Mazzini's *Young Italy* became their political Bible. The resurgence of nationalism in Turkey, China and Persia provided them with models they could imitate. The methods of the Sinn Fein in Ireland showed the way. Japan's victory over Russia (1905) filled them with the hope that if one Asian people could triumph over a European power, why not another?

What was the Indian Muslims' reaction to the frenzied impatience of the radicals to grab power?

At one end there were the die-hard Wahabis mourning the passing of India from *Dar-ul-Islam* to the British-dominated *Dar-ul-Harab*. So great was the hatred of these people against the British that while they had condoned Maratha domination over India, they rejected everything foreign and preached resumption of war against the British. This group used the Delhi College to influence religious-minded Muslims in the Uttar Pradesh, Bihar and Bengal.

Diametrically opposed to the Wahabi line of thinking was the Aligarh School founded by Syed Ahmed Khan (1817-98). As a paid employee of the East India Company, Syed had kept aloof from the Mutiny. Two years after the Mutiny had been crushed he persuaded 15,000 Muslims to pledge loyalty to the British crown. "British rule," said Syed Ahmed, "is the most wonderful phenomenon the world has ever seen." The admiration became mutual. In Syed Ahmed, the English rulers saw the means of keeping educated Muslims away from the Hindu nationalists. In return, Syed Ahmed looked to the British to see that, while introducing democratic institutions in India, they did not reduce the Muslim minority to subservience of the Hindus but maintained its distinct entity and its culture – notably the continuance of Urdu against the demand for making Hindi the national language of India. His journal, *Tahzib al Akhlaq* (Civilisation and Culture), written in simple, colloquial Urdu, warned Indian Muslims of the consequences of their joining the National Congress. Syed Ahmed was primarily an educationist. In 1875 he was able to muster enough support to set up the Anglo-Mohammedan Oriental College at Aligarh. Aligarh soon became the centre for preaching Muslim separatism.

Syed Ahmed's pro-British views aroused much criticism but his adherence to religious ritual and his dedication to the service of the community silenced his critics. His scholarship won him many admirers. His *Azar al Sanadid* is to this day regarded as the most reliable account of the history and monuments of Delhi. He described himself as a "naturalist" (*nehehari*) and propagated the belief that "between the word of God and the works of God (nature) there can be no contradiction."

Syed Ahmed got the Muslim elite behind him. Two well-known figures were from Hyderabad State: Chiragh Ali and Mahdi Ali Khan (1837-1907). Mahadi Ali Khan resigned from the Congress to become Secretary of the Anglo-Mohammedan Oriental College at Aligarh. He rejected both Pan-Islamism and Indian nationalism and instead espoused the cause of separate nationhood for the Muslims of India. Amongst the most outstanding of Syed Ahmed's supporters was Amir Ali, the author of *A Short History of the Saracens* (1889) and *The Spirit of Islam* (1992). Also clambering on Syed Ahmed's bandwagon were two eminent poets of the Urdu language: Altaf Hussain Hali who in 1879, at Syed Ahmed's request, composed the *mussaddas madd-e-jaz-I-Islam* – an impassioned composition on the ebb and flow of Islam, and Akbar Allahbadi (1846-1921) who, while lampooning the Anglicised wog in some of the most humourous and biting satire written in Urdu, remained an ardent admirer of Muslim regeneration as envisaged by Syed Ahmed.

The educated elite, while holding fast to the tenets of Islam, exhorted Muslims to take to Western learning and thus made the traditionalists of the Delhi Wahabi School (and their counterparts in Lucknow, Khairabad and later Deoband) appear like Mullahs screaming obscurantism from the tops of antiquated minarets. Although the Deoband School attained an eminence rivaling that of Al Azhar of Cairo, its diatribes against the Aligarh School ("Deadly poison for Islam," said

Rashid Ahmed Gangohi) failed to enthuse any but the most devout of Muslim purists.

There were some in Aligarh who could not stomach the unabashed anglophilism of Syed Ahmed. There were also some in Deoband who believed that teaching Muslim theology was not enough. The two groups joined together to set up in 1919 the Jamia Millia Islamia, a nationalist Muslim University, at Okhla, on the outskirts of Delhi.

It was in this setting that the British introduced the first important measure to induct Indians into the administration of their country. In 1905 the Liberal Party won the elections in England and Lord Morley was made Secretary of State. The Viceroy, Lord Minto, was, however, a Conservative. The Morley-Minto Reforms which were later enshrined in an Act of Parliament, provided for the nomination of an Indian to the Viceroy's executive council, an increase in the number of elected members in the central and state legislatures and more portfolios to be handled by elected Indians. These were significant steps towards self-government. However, at the same time a wedge was driven between the Hindus and the Muslims. Muslims were encouraged to put forward claims for separate constituencies (where only Muslims could vote for Muslim candidates) and for weightages so that the smallness of their numbers would be offset by greater representation in the legislative bodies and the services. Both these demands were eagerly conceded by the British.

Soon after the annulment of the partition of Bengal, propaganda was mounted to make the annulment appear as a concession to Hindu nationalism. The Morley-Minto Reforms and reunification of Bengal were an exposition of the time-worn principle of government: *divide et impera* in all its naked crudity.

World War I (1914-18) was an important landmark in the history of India's freedom movement. It marked the zenith of Indian loyalty to Britain (1,200,000 Indians fought for the British; 26,000 fell in the battlefields of France, Turkey and Africa; 70,000 were wounded). Indian princes and industrialists opened up their coffers; nationalists put aside their aspirations and helped in the war effort; men like Gandhi volunteered for service in the Red Cross. Hindu and Muslim leaders got together and in December 1916 signed a pact at Lucknow to iron out their differences. Even the British felt that they owed India something for its unqualified support in Britain's years of peril. In the August of 1917, when the tide of war had begun to turn in their favour, Lord Montagu, Secretary of State for India, made, what appeared to everyone, a momentous declaration promising Indians a status equal to that enjoyed by the other dominions – Canada, South Africa, Australia and New Zealand. It provided for "the increasing association of Indians in every branch of the administration and the gradual development of self-governing institutions with a view to the progressive realisation of responsible government in India as an integral part of the Empire".

Indians had reason to hope and prepare themselves for freedom.

With the end of the war came the great disillusionment. Indians heard of the shabby treatment given to Sikh emigrants in Canada and the United States. The most shameful was the episode of the Japanese vessel *Komagata Maru* – chartered by Indian emigrants in 1914. It was turned back by the Canadian authorities and on its return, a fracas at Budge Budge harbour resulted in the killing of thirty-one Sikhs; details of the incident were suppressed and only came to be known after the war. Conditions under which Indian soldiers had to serve on the front also caused much resentment. Then, the harsh treaty proposed to be imposed on the defeated Turks inflamed Indian Muslim sentiment. An outbreak of the flu in epidemic form and a series of bad harvests added to the miseries of the people. British retraction of some of their wartime promises, followed by the imposition of measures to repress agitation, was enough to bring the simmering discontent to the boil.

Gandhi, who had already become a celebrity for his successful passive resistance movement in South Africa, now arrived on the Indian scene.

15

Freedom Movement-2

The Gandhian Decades

The twenty-seven years between the ending of the two world wars (1918-45) could without exaggeration be described as the three decades of Gandhi. He was the philosopher of the freedom movement, the field marshal of its army of passive resisters, the visiting British statesmen. He became the voice of India. India came to be known as the land of Gandhi and Gandhi became India's spiritual mentor (Guru), saint (Mahatma) and a father (Bapu), all rolled into one.

Gandhi was born on 2 October 1869 at Porbandar, a princely state in western India. His father was in the employ of the ruling family. Though the Gandhis were orthodox Hindus of the Bania (trading) caste, they were friendly with Muslims and Zoroastrians. They were puritans who not only abhorred liquor, tobacco and meat but regarded abstemiousness as a virtue.

Mahatma Gandhi

Gandhi was schooled in his home town. At thirteen, a marriage was arranged for him. At eighteen, he became a father. After schooling he was shipped off to England to study for the bar (1888-91). For a short while he tried to anglicise himself. He took lessons in elocution and ballroom dancing. But he soon gave up this futile attempt and, as often happens to Indians when they go abroad, he became more conscious of his Indian heritage, history and culture. He read the Gita and the life and teachings of the Buddha in English translations. Being religiously inclined, he read the Bible and was thrilled by the Sermon on the Mount. He read Carlyle's *Heroes and Hero Worship*. Having got his barrister's diploma from the Inner Temple and sampled a little of the Western style of living, he came back home to set up practice in his home town. His foray into law was a flop: at his first appearance at court, he failed to open his mouth and returned the fee to his client.

Some time later he was engaged by a Muslim firm to represent its interests in cases pending in South Africa. He became a "coolie barrister". It was in South Africa that Gandhi's attention was diverted from the practice of law to protest against the vile treatment meted out by the white racist regime to the Asian emigrant communities and the black natives. Gandhi writes about an incident that was a turning-point in his career. He had a first-class ticket but a white man objected to sharing his compartment with Gandhi. "I was pushed out of the train by a police-constable at Maritzburg, and the train having left, was sitting in the room, shivering in the cold. I did not know where my luggage was nor did I care to enquire from anybody, lest I might be insulted and assaulted once again. Sleep was out of the question. Doubt took possession of my mind. Late at night I came to the conclusion that to run back to India would be cowardly. I must accomplish what I had undertaken."

Gandhi drifted away from legal practice. He appeared in the law courts not as an attorney but as an accused person. In the twenty years he spent in South Africa (1893-1914) he was imprisoned four times and on many occasions manhandled by the police and by his own countrymen. The South African experience made Gandhi turn to pacifism. He read Thoreau and Tolstoy. He came to believe that people should live in small self-sustaining communities and set up ashrams (Phoenix, and later, Tolstoy farm) where men and women cooked their own food and spun yarn. He read Ruskin's *Unto This Last* and made the Gita his book of daily prayer. In Thoreau's notions in *Civil Disobedience* he found the answer to his political problems. Hinduism extolled the virtues of *ahimsa* – non-violence. So he made *ahimsa* his creed, civil disobedience his weapon and *satyagraha* (truth-force) the way of wielding it.

All this is stated in Gandhi's autobiography, *My Experiments with Truth*. It is not great literature, as is often stated by Gandhians; it is the confession of an honest, outspoken man of great courage. What strikes one about the *Experiments* is its stark candour. Gandhi, the vegetarian, swallowing meat and throwing it up; Gandhi, the puritan, visiting a brothel; Gandhi donning a dinner-jacket and trying to learn how to waltz; Gandhi the lusty youth, stealing away from his sick father's bedside to copulate with his young wife – and being forever guilt-ridden because his father happened to die while he was thus engaged; Gandhi at thirty-seven, without consulting his wife, taking a vow of lifelong continence – and thereafter exposing himself to temptation to make sure that he was in full control of his "baser" desires; Gandhi, the faddist, refusing to let doctors treat his ailing son and instead trying out mud-packs and prayer as cures. The *Experiments* makes amusing, often irritating, reading. But in the end the reader does not find himself smiling in superior disdain but convinced that what he has read is the tortuous soul-searching of an unusually honest man. There was nothing startlingly original about Gandhian philosophy. Many aspects of it were borrowed from popular Hinduism. *Ahimsa* (non-violence) had for centuries been the *paramo dharma* (primary law) of the Jains and other Hindu sects. Hindu *bhaktas* had decried the practice of untouchability. European philosophers had dreamt of a Utopia of self-contained village republics where people lived simple lives by reducing their needs to the necessary minimum. Many Indians before him had preached the use of *swadeshi* (made in one's own country) goods and the boycott of foreign products. They had also talked of *swaraj* (self-rule) as the birthright of every man. Gandhi's chief contribution was to put all these concepts together into a coherent philosophic-ethical-political system and to become the living embodiment of all he preached.

By the end of 1913 Gandhi had won most of his South African battles. He had the good fortune to have as his chief adversary, General Smuts, who was a Christian and a gentleman. Although Smuts repeatedly gaoled Gandhi and thousands of his supporters, Gandhi bore him no ill-will. He presented Smuts with a pair of sandals he had stitched while in gaol. Smuts acknowledged the gift with a generous compliment to the donor. "I have worn these sandals for many a summer since then, even though I may feel that I am not worthy to stand in the shoes of so great a man," he wrote.

After a short sojourn in England Gandhi returned home to India early in 1915. Earlier he had accepted Gokhale's suggestion that he should keep away from politics for a year and spend the time getting re-acquainted with the country. He was acclaimed by his countrymen as the new messiah – "the great soul (Mahatma) in a begger's garb", as the poet Tagore described him.

Gandhi raised an ashram on the banks of the Sabarmati a few miles upstream from Ahmedabad, and named it the Satyagraha Ashram. Its twenty-five inmates were obliged to conform to Gandhi's views of life; apart from the pledge of *ahimsa* and manual labour to feed and clothe oneself, it also included the vow of chastity.

Gandhi shed everything Western: he began to dress in a scanty dhoti and sandals as did the peasants of India. At the opening ceremony of the Benares Hindu University he protested at being asked to speak in a foreign language (English) and told the coterie of princelings attending the function to strip themselves of their pomp and finery.

A year later he had the opportunity to try out *satyagraha* in Bihar. He deliberately defied an order to keep out of Champaran district where peasants had complained of unjust treatment by white indigo planters. The prohibitory order was withdrawn. Gandhi repeated the experiment to get a fair deal for the textile workers of Ahmedabad. This time he threatened to fast unto death unless the workers' demands were conceded. They were. A third time he used *satyagraha* to compel the Government to remit land tax to the impoverished peasantry in Kheda district in Gujarat.

Gandhi was not consistent in his pacifism. He organised an ambulance unit for the British in the Boer war, helped the administration in suppressing the Zulu rebellion, helped recruitment in the first world war, attended a war conference presided over by the viceroy and voted for increased war effort. He had a habit of preaching non-violence to others, even when it was absurdly impractical. For instance, he asked the Jews to resist Hitler passively. "If one Jew or all the Jews," he wrote, "were to accept the prescription (civil resistance) here offered, he or they cannot be worse off than now. And suffering voluntarily undergone, will bring them an inner strength and joy which no number of resolutions of sympathy passed in the world outside Germany can. I am convinced that, if someone with courage and vision can arise among them to lead them in non-violent action, the winter of their despair can, in the twinkling of an eye, be turned into the summer of hope."

Yet, when India fought Pakistan in Kashmir in 1947 and forcibly took over Hyderabad, Gandhi defended the Indian action. Charitably, this can be seen as the contradictions that exist in all great men.

Gandhi rose to supreme eminence as the leader of the Indian masses in the turmoil that followed World

War I. The Government, instead of soothing the people's nerves, clamped down strict censorship. The notorious Rowlatt Bills were designed to empower the administration to detain people without trial and try them without jury or legal representation.

Gandhi led the agitation against the Rowlatt Bills. He called for a general *hartal* – cessation from work. The *hartal* intended by Gandhi to be peaceful did not remain so. In Ahmedabad a policeman was murdered. Gandhi confessed that, "a rapier run through my body could hardly have pained me more," and called off the *hartal*. He punished himself by undertaking a three-day fast. While Gandhi was purging his conscience for what his followers had done, the authorities reacted in exactly the opposite way. At Amritsar an assemblage of peasants who had come from outlying villages to attend the Baisakhi (spring) fair (13 April, 1919) and most of whom knew nothing of an order forbidding assemblies of five or more, was "dispersed" by machine-gun fire, leaving over 400 dead and over 2000 wounded. The shooting was followed by the imposition of curfew which prevented succour being brought to the dying. Martial law was imposed over the province, many towns and villages were bombed from the air, suspects were flogged in public; and in a street in Amritsar, where a European had been murdered, citizens were forced to crawl on their bellies.

The massacre of Jallianwala Bagh at Amritsar and the tyranny of martial law turned India against the

British. The masses turned to Gandhi; a few hotheads turned to violence.

Gandhi was not above exploiting situations which suited his general purpose. He had noticed that Indian Muslims were generally cool towards the freedom movement led by the Congress because of its Hindu orientation. He wanted to gain their confidence and get them to form a united front. He saw that they were agitated over the dismemberment of the Turkish Empire and had organised the *Khilafat* movement to protest against it. Although he could not have had any enthusiasm for the caliph (the Turks under Kemal Pasha abolished the caliphate), Gandhi espoused its cause by attending the Muslim conference in Delhi (November 1919) and assuring the Muslims of support in a non-cooperation movement against the British.

Indian Muslims joined Gandhi. Thus strengthened, Gandhi asked Indians who had received honours or awards from the British to turn them in. Thus did Gandhi, the Anglophile of 1918 turn an Anglophobe a year later and denounce the British Government as "Satanic".

From 1920 onwards Gandhi was everywhere; his croaking, lisping voice was heard by millions of people. For the first time women in their hundreds of thousands joined his *satyagraha*. To the educated, he spoke through his two weeklies, *Young India* and *Navjeevan*.

Along with his crusade against British rule, he campaigned to reform Indian society. Perhaps his greatest achievement in this respect was his denunciation of the practice of untouchability.

"I regard untouchability as the greatest blot on Hinduism," he wrote. "Untouchability has degraded us, made us the pariahs of the (British) Empire. What crimes, for which we condemn the (British) Government as satanic, have not we been guilty of towards our untouchable brethren?" Gandhi gave the untouchables a new name – Harijan, the children of God. He would wash the feet of Harijans in his ashram – an unheard of thing in those days – and insist that the other high-class ashramites follow suit. Untouchability still exists in India, though it is banned by law. But Gandhi, more than anyone else, reduced its virulence and brought the seventy million Harijans closer into the mainstream of Indian life. Yet, strangely enough, Gandhi obliquely supported the Hindu caste system.

Of dubious value, however, was Gandhi's campaign against alcohol. He believed that drink was an unmitigated evil and prohibition was for the good of the industrial worker and the peasant who would otherwise be tempted to spend a large part of their meagre income on alcohol. "It is the factory labourers and others that drink," he wrote. "They are forlorn, uncared for, and they take to drink."

Gandhi's views on alcohol were officially adopted by the Government after independence and prohibition was made one of the Directive Principles of State

Policy. It was tried out in most of the states but found to be unworkable. The poor continued to drink and poison themselves with illicit liquor. Today, only one state – Gujarat – enforces a watered down policy of prohibition.

Gandhi also attacked the institution of child marriage and championed women's equality in *Young India*. "This custom of child marriage is both a moral and a physical evil," he wrote. And on the segregation of women: "Why is there all this morbid anxiety about female purity? Have women any say in the matter of male purity? We hear nothing of women's anxiety about men's chastity. Why should men arrogate to themselves the right to regulate female purity?"

These words sound almost like today's Women's Lib and they help to explain why so many Indian women joined Gandhi.

But let us go back to Gandhi's role in the independence movement. The 1919 Rowlatt Act – which had precipitated the Amritsar massacre – had provided for a commission of inquiry after ten years to review the working of the Act. This Commission, headed by Sir John Simon, a die-hard Conservative, arrived in India in 1927. The Congress made it quite clear that it felt insulted by the Commission and boycotted it. The Commission, however, toured the country despite the protests. In one such demonstration, Lala Lajpat Rai, the Punjabi nationalist, received a blow from a policeman and died soon afterwards.

This period also saw the growth of Muslim separatism. Jinnah began increasingly to dissociate himself from the views of the Congress and became the dominant figure in the Muslim League. He demanded a federal constitution in which Muslim majority areas would have complete autonomy. Jinnah's disenchantment with the Congress was not a little due to his dislike – the feeling was mutual – of Nehru.

In the summer of 1929 a Labour administration came to power in Britain and the new Prime Minister declared the Government's intention of making India a self-governing dominion within the Commonwealth. Lord Irwin, the viceroy, however, refused to give such an assurance and the stage was set for Gandhi's next act of civil disobedience. He felt that to rouse the masses, it was futile to talk to them about dominion status. An easily recognisable symbol was needed. The intuitive genius that he was, he hit upon the salt tax.

The Government controlled the production of salt and in 1930 half the retail price of salt represented tax. As everybody bought and ate salt, what better way to rouse them than to ask them to make their own salt? Thus began the great Salt March. Along with seventy-eight ashramites Gandhi set off on a two-hundred-mile walk from Ahmedabad to Dandi. The walk took twenty-nine days and brought the entire nation to an unprecedented pitch of excitement and awareness. The march also riveted the attention of the world to the Indian independence movement. On 5 April, Gandhi symbolically picked up some salt from the sea and thousands followed suit by making salt illegally. Soon afterwards Gandhi was arrested.

The British Government tried to break the impasse by holding a Round Table Conference, representing Indian interests including the princes, in London. Gandhi was released from jail and went to London to attend the conference. But nothing was achieved and Gandhi returned to Bombay. Resentment against the British led to an outbreak of terrorism and communal violence. Gandhi's restraining influence seemed to be declining, while Jinnah's stature with the Muslims grew.

Under the Government of India Act of 1935 elections were held for popular responsible government in the provinces. The results came as a shock to the Congress: though it won in the Hindu majority areas, it could not claim to speak for all the Muslims. Congress ministries came to power in some provinces and a struggle followed within the Congress between Subhas Chandra Bose, the fiery Bengali nationalist, and Gandhi. At first Gandhi tried to convert Bose, the revolutionary who believed in violence. But with Bose's election as President of the Congress in 1939 an unbridgeable split developed between the two men. Bose was eventually forced to leave the Congress and start a new leftwing organisation, the Forward Bloc.

With the outbreak of World War II, the contradictions of British rule in India surfaced: Indians were asked to help fight Hitler and save democracy, but were denied it at home. Gandhi's instinct, which was not shared by Nehru and other Congress leaders, however, was to give Britain support in the war. Bose was at the other extreme. He fled the country and joined hands with the Axis powers to form the Indian National Army, composed of Indian POW's captured by the Japanese. It was also during the war that Jinnah's ideas about Pakistan began to crystallise, though he did not conceive of a completely independent country.

With the whole of South-East Asia falling to the Japanese, the British sent a mission to India, headed by Sir Stafford Cripps, to appease Indian opinion and rally the country behind the Government. Cripps more or less conceded Indian independence, the only proviso being the guarantee of "British obligations". With the Japanese knocking at the gates of India, the British were in a weak position and, not surprisingly, the mission failed. Gandhi and the whole Congress Working Committee were arrested. The demonstrations that followed were put down with a severe hand. Attention now shifted to Bose and the INA. His rallying cry "Jai Hind!" electrified the nation. But Bose's success depended on the Japanese and as the fortunes of war turned against them, his cause was doomed.

Events moved rapidly after the war. With a Labour Government in power, Indian independence was only a question of time. The British wanted to relegate Gandhi to the background and deal more with Nehru and Jinnah. The events of the next three years were, therefore, dominated by these two antagonistic personalities.

Lord Wavell, the well-meaning but somewhat inept viceroy, was replaced by Lord Mountbatten. The deadline for the transfer of power was put forward and elections were held all over India. The communal issue came to the surface and Jinnah's Muslim League scored stunning victories in the Muslim majority areas. For the first time the concept of an independent Pakistan began to be taken seriously. A Cabinet mission was sent by Prime Minister Attlee to study the situation. The mission obliquely recommended a partition of the subcontinent, thus setting the scene for the communal violence that soon erupted.

With a mutiny in the Indian Navy and unrest in the other services, the Government panicked and drew up a plan for partition. Pakistan was virtually being presented to Jinnah on a platter. During this period Gandhi kept away from the scene of negotiations. He refused to accept a truncated India and toured the country trying to douse the fires of communal passion.

Independence came on 15 August 1947 but Gandhi refused to take part in the celebrations. When the riots continued in Delhi, Gandhi went on another of his many fasts on 13 January 1948. He ended it on 18 January after a pledge from various organisations representing Hindus and Muslims that they would keep the peace. On 30 January during one of his prayer meetings, a thirty-five-year old man called Nathuram Godse came up to him, bowed and fired at point blank range. Gandhi fell and died with the words, *Hey Ram* – "Oh, God" on his lips.

16

Nehru

*N*ext to Gandhi, the most important person that India produced in recent times was Jawaharlal Nehru. What Paul did in building the Church of Christ for Christendom, Nehru did in shaping the country which Gandhi had led to freedom. Perhaps a better analogy would be to say that what Stalin was to Lenin, or Chiang and Mao to Sun Yat Sen, Nehru was to Gandhi – the builder and the architect. But a builder with a design of his own.

Before we study what Nehru did we should acquaint ourselves with who Nehru was and what made him what he became.

Nehru was the eldest child and the only son of a very prosperous lawyer-politician, Motilal, who practised law at the High Court of Allahabad. The Nehrus were Saraswat Brahmins from Kashmir: some forefather of theirs had at some time been engaged in the digging of a canal (*nahr*); thereafter his descendants took on the family name Nehru – canal-makers. The family migrated from Kashmir to Agra and from Agra to Allahabad. The Nehru family's fortunes were made by Motilal. Much is said about the aristocratic origins of the family. This is largely to magnify the greatness of Jawaharlal who, as the Indian cliché goes, "sacrificed his all at the altar of his motherland". The Nehrus were a middle-class family which came into a lot of money.

Jawaharlal was born on the 14 November 1889. At the time, his father was on the make and had already moved from the "native quarter" of the city to the "Civil Lines" (so named because English civilians lived there). Later, Motilal, whose clientele now included some of the wealthiest landowners (and as landowners have litigation in their blood), built himself a palatial house "Anand Bhavan" – the Abode of Bliss. It was in this house that young Jawaharlal and his two sisters were reared by hordes

Jawaharlal Nehru

of servants and a succession of English nannies. Since many of the senior Nehru's clients and friends were Muslims and Englishmen, the younger Nehru's Brahminism was tempered by Muslim and European influences.

Motilal wanted to make his son a wog (Westernised Oriental gentleman) who would get an *entrée* into English officialdom. When the boy was fifteen he was sent to Harrow. And after two years at this prestigious English public school, to Trinity College, Cambridge. Young Nehru got a second class in Natural Sciences in his tripos, which is the Cambridge University equivalent of a degree. He also attended meetings of Fabian Socialists.

As was customary amongst Indians studying in English universities at the time, young Nehru also enrolled himself at the Inner Temple to become a barrister. After three years of wining and dining at the Inns of Court – the study of law was not imperative and examinations were a formality – Nehru was called to the bar, i.e., given a licence to practise law. In 1912 at the age of twenty three Jawaharlal returned to Allahabad with BA (Cantab), Barrister-at-Law appended to his name.

For a while Motilal toyed with the idea of getting his son into the Indian Civil Service. Jawaharlal did not agree. Motilal got his son to work in his office and to help him prepare his briefs. Young Nehru showed no particular aptitude for law and was content to appear in court as a junior to his father. He was more drawn to politics. He attended meetings of the Indian National Congress and became a member of its provincial branch. When World War I broke out Jawaharlal Nehru raised funds for Indian settlers in South Africa and for indentured labourers in the Fiji Islands.

In 1916 Nehru married Kamala Kaul. A year later, on 19 November 1917, was born their only child, Indira Priyadarshini, a future Prime Minister of India.

At the end of the war, Jawaharlal Nehru emerged from the silken cocoon of Anand Bhavan. The massacre of Amritsar and the atrocities committed by the martial law administrators in the Punjab came as a traumatic shock to Nehru. He lost faith in Britain's sense of justice. When Gandhi called for *satyagraha*, Nehru responded, "I was afire with enthusiasm and wanted to join ... immediately,", he wrote. "I hardly thought of the consequences – law-breaking, jail-going, etc., and if I thought of them I did not care." His father threatened to throw him out of the house if he joined Gandhi. It was an idle threat, because Motilal was himself a friend and disciple of Gandhi and agreed to preside over the session of the Indian National Congress which met in Amritsar, the very city where the massacre had taken place.

Were the people ready for freedom? Jawaharlal went out to the villages to find out the answer for himself. In 1920 the city-bred, anglicised Nehru made his first contact with the countryside. "I was filled with shame and sorrow," he wrote. "Shame at my own easy-going and comfortable life and our petty politics of the city which ignored this vast multitude of semi-naked sons and daughters of India. A new picture of India seemed to rise before me, naked, starving, crushed and utterly miserable." (*Toward Freedom*, pp 56-57.)

The personality of Gandhi made a deep and abiding impact on the mind of Nehru. For a while Nehru thought of becoming an ascetic. He gave up smoking (he took it up five years later) and eating meat and, despite being an agnostic, began to read the Bhagvad Gita. Although he was irritated by Gandhi's obscurantism and impatient with his esoteric references to the "Inner Voice", he continued to respect him to the point of worship. He came to look upon Gandhi as his father and guru. In return, Gandhi began to treat Nehru as his favourite son and made sure that after him the mantle of leadership fell on Nehru's shoulders.

Another important factor in moulding Nehru's personality was his experience of prison life. He was gaoled nine times and spent a total of nine years in different Indian jails. These years gave him time to read, write and meditate on the political and economic problems of the country, Almost all his major writings, like *Glimpses of World History* – a series of essays in the form of letters written for the edification of his daughter – *The Discovery of India* and his *Autobiography* were written in prison.

They are not works of original research, nor, as is often noised by the Nehru clique, of great literary significance, but they do reflect considerable erudition and are an exercise in clearing of the mind. His wide reading put him intellectually well above the run of contemporary Indian politicians. In some ways he came to symbolise the Platonic concept of a philosopher-king.

In the fervently patriotic atmosphere that prevailed, prison-going provided Nehru with a halo of martyrdom. Wildly exaggerated stories of the family millions, the blueness of its aristocratic blood began to circulate. Here was a man who had been at school with the Prince of Wales! Who sent his washing to Paris! And who could hold his own with the intellectual elite of Europe! The world was his oyster but his heart was with the downtrodden peasants and workers!

Nehru had things to say about "the rising tide of Imperialism of the United States", then in evidence in Latin America. But Nehru did not go all the way with the communists. He was willing to come to terms with Imperialist Great Britain if India was given Dominion Status. Communists accused both Gandhi and Nehru of "betrayal of the cause of workers and peasants".

In 1927, Nehru went on a long-delayed pilgrimage to the Soviet Union on the occasion of its tenth anniversary. He had come determined to be impressed; and was duly impressed with all that he saw on a brief four-day guided tour of Moscow and its environs. He published his starry-eyed eulogy of the Soviet system, but his reasons for counselling friendship towards

Russia were pragmatic. He wrote: "She is our neighbour, a powerful neighbour, which may be friendly to us and cooperate with us, or may be a thorn in our side. In either event we have to know her and understand her and shape our policy accordingly."

Gandhi was not impressed by Nehru's enthusiasm for socialism because he believed that the socialist method, class struggle, ran counter to the spirit of *satyagraha* – non-violent non-cooperation. When Nehru moved a resolution in October 1927 at the Madras session of the Congress in favour of "complete national independence" (instead of Dominion Status), Gandhi chided him for reducing deliberations of the Congress to "the level of a schoolboy's debating society". (Tendulkar, Vol II, p 402). "You are going too fast," wrote Gandhi to Nehru. "You should have taken time to think and get acclimatised." And a few weeks later Gandhi accused Nehru of carrying on "open warfare" against him.

Although Nehru never turned his back on socialism, he was careful enough not to alienate the Mahatma. Others, notably his rival for power, Subhas Chandra Bose, crossed swords with Gandhi and were forced to commit political *harakiri*.

In 1928 Nehru became president of the All India Trade Union Congress. The same year a serious split took place in the Congress party over the Nehru (Motilal) Report. Gandhi wanted the report to be accepted. Bose wanted it to be rejected. Although

Jawaharlal Nehru was inclined to accept Bose's point of view, he was tactful enough to maintain a façade of neutrality. Gandhi rewarded Nehru for not openly going over to Bose by assuring him of his support in the years to come. "In bravery, Nehru is not to be surpassed," wrote the Mahatma. "Who can excel him in love of the country? He is pure as crystal, he is truthful beyond suspicion ... the nation is safe in his hands." What more could the "Father of the Nation" have done to intimate to his countrymen who he thought best fitted to succeed him?

Nehru held his socialism in check for some time. The test of loyalty came over the trial at Meerut of thirty-two communists charged with sedition and conspiracy. Like the Nationalists, Nehru expressed sympathy for the men after making it abundantly clear that he was a nationalist first, a socialist second and a communist never.

Gandhi never let Nehru down. He even came round to Nehru's view that India should strive for complete independence (*purna swaraj*) instead of Dominion Status. At the momentous session of the Congress at Lahore in December 1929, Nehru was elected president. He gave a new dimension to the freedom movement.

He emphasised the need to placate the fears of the minorities and win them over to the Congress. He drew attention to the repression of the people's movements in the princely states, the wretched plight of India's peasantry and the rapidly growing industrial proletariat. He went further and expressed agreement with leftist radicals. "Violence is bad, but slavery is worse," he said. "Success comes to those who dare and act; it seldom goes to the timid who are afraid of the consequences." In one swoop Nehru captured the hearts of the Gandhian conservatives, the peasants and workers and the impatient youth of the country. The ten years, 1920-30, saw Nehru emerge as the leader of India – second only to Gandhi. His chief critics were the communists who denounced him as "the most harmful and dangerous obstacle to victory of the Indian revolution".

The civil disobedience movement following Gandhi's salt *satyagraha* in March-April 1930 saw Nehru (and 10,000 other Indians) in jail. He was let out on parole for a brief period of eight days to attend to his sick father. This time the proud father organised mass celebrations on 14 November as a birthday gift for his son. The Government retaliated by putting another 5,000 nationalists, including Nehru's wife, Kamala, in jail.

Nehru utilised this period in jail to write a series of letter-essays, *Glimpses of World History*, for his daughter.

The Congress session of 1931 at Karachi was presided over by Nehru's chief rival, Sardar Patel. At this session Nehru sponsored a resolution which spelt out his ideas on the kind of government India should have when it achieved independence. He proposed a constitution which would guarantee citizens freedom of speech, association and religious practice; justice and equality of opportunity and "a living wage"; limited hours of work, insurance to cover old age, disability and unemployment. Included in this portmanteau full of pious resolutions were also items from Gandhi's list: prohibition, patronage of handspun *khadi* cloth and others taken from the socialist textbook: "The state shall own or control key industries and services, mineral resources, railways, waterways, shipping and other means of public transport."

Nehru was the only leader who looked ahead to the future. The Karachi constitutional proposals were mooted by him sixteen years before India became free; and he was talking of the "socialist pattern of society" twenty-four years before it was formally adopted as the objective of the Congress party at the Avadi session in 1955.

During the Round Table Conference in London, which was attended by Gandhi as the sole representative of the Congress Party, Nehru stayed behind and organised a "no-tax campaign" amongst the Uttar Pradesh peasantry. He was gaoled for the sixth time. During this period of imprisonment, Nehru reflected on the state of affairs preceding World War II. Mussolini had seized power in Italy; Hitler was on the make in Germany; a military junta was running Japan and had annexed Manchuria. Western democracies were retreating before the onslaught of fascism. The only nation standing up against it was the Soviet Union. Although Nehru did not like Stalin's methods, he could not help admiring the Soviet system. He wrote: "I do believe that fundamentally the choice before the world today is between some form of communism and some form of fascism, and I am all for the former, i.e., communism ...There is no middle road ... and I choose the communist ideal ... I think that these methods will have to adapt themselves to changing conditions and may vary in different countries."

While Gandhi was engaged in fighting the Communal Award made by the British and fasting for "self-purification", Nehru was engrossed in his studies and in nursing his tubercular wife. During a brief period of freedom given to him to arrange for her treatment, he made more inflammatory speeches for which he had to suffer another two years in jail. His wife's health deteriorated. Immediately on his release he took her to Switzerland for treatment. It was of no avail. Kamala Nehru died in a sanatorium in Lausanne in Switzerland on 28 February 1936.

Nehru spent a few weeks in Europe and saw nazism and fascism at close quarters. He was filled with revulsion at their racist and colonial policies. On his way back home he had the pleasure of turning down Mussolini's invitation for a meeting.

The scene in India had changed. The Government of India Act of 1935 had been passed by the British Parliament. The socialist wing of the Congress led by Jaya Prakash Narayan was for rejecting it outright. The conservatives were for accepting it and then wrecking it. Nehru became the bridge between the two factions. He kept up a posture of radicalism by publicly snubbing the conservatives. At the Lucknow session, where he presided, he packed the Working Committee with radicals and forced the conservatives to resign. Gandhi was angry with him: "Under your rebukes and magisterial manner and above all your arrogation of what has appeared to them your infallibility and superior knowledge, they have resigned. They feel that you have treated them with scant courtesy and never defended them from socialists' ridicule and even misrepresentations." (Nehru, *A Bunch of Old Letters*, p 183).

Nehru's Machiavellianism paid off. He played the two factions against each other and ensured his staying at the helm of the Congress at a most crucial time in its history. As President of the party, he organised the election campaign. He covered 50,000 miles and spoke to 10 million people. The result was a resounding victory for the Congress and for Nehru. Of the 1,585 seats, the Congress party won 711. It gained an absolute majority in 5 of India's 11 provinces and was the largest single party in three others.

The triumph went to Nehru's head and that of the Congress party. The euphoria was somewhat premature; the new constitution, though a big step towards self-government, did by no means eliminate British presence in India. Nehru talked of sovereign power. He made statements on the language problem (which were later proved to be fallacious) and set up a National Planning Committee to draft a programme for the economic and social regeneration of the country. In fixing his gaze on a yet distant Shangri-la of free India, Nehru overlooked or deliberately ignored the rising tide of Muslim separatism.

The Muslim League made a very poor showing in the 1937 elections. To make up for the losses at the polls, it took desperate steps to rally Muslim opinion by raising the bogey of a Hindu-Congress conspiracy to persecute the Muslims. It published a charge-sheet (The Pirpur Report), which was a hodge-podge of fact and horror stories of Hindu oppression of Muslims. Nehru considered it beneath him to take notice of it; the Muslims did not.

In 1938 Nehru was in Europe once more. Civil war between the elected government and the rebel fascists had broken out in Spain. The Nazis' "barbarian feet" trampling over Austria had countenanced nothing more from the Western democracies than wordy apathy. Nehru returned home more than ever convinced that the only hope of the free world was socialism, presided over by the Soviet Union. Later that year he spent some days in China as a guest of Marshal Chiang Kai-shek. Visions of a free, united and powerful Asian bloc founded on Sino-Indian friendship loomed before his eyes. Yet another dimension was added to his ever expanding horizon.

Nehru seldom let these grandiose dreams of a socialist Valhalla blur his sight to the immediate problems of keeping the leadership of the country in his own hands. At the time two men threatened his position: Sardar Patel, a dour-faced Gujarati conservative who had earned the sobriquet "iron dictator"; and the flamboyant Bengali radical, Subhas Bose. Of the two, Bose was the more serious contender for power. He was younger than Nehru, academically as well-equipped and with as great a vision of the future. Bose was a more gifted orator, with more daring, and endowed with an uncanny wizardry of making everything he did appear spectacular.

The way Nehru settled Bose's hash was masterly. At the Congress session at Tripuri in the December of 1938, Bose had the temerity to pitch himself against the Gandhians. Although Nehru's views were the same as Bose's he knew that no one could cross Gandhi's path without paying a heavy price for it. Nehru expressed sympathy with Bose's viewpoint but stuck to Gandhi. Bose had a momentary triumph; he defeated Gandhi's candidate in the contest for presidency. But within a few months Gandhi mustered his forces and compelled Bose to resign. Bose formed a separate party, the Forward Bloc, which never amounted to very much.

By the summer of 1939 Hitler was ready to unleash his army on Europe. The Congress party defined its attitude to the conflict that was a about to take place. It placed on record its abhorrence of fascism but at the same time warned Great Britain that it must not take Indian support for granted. Britain must make a declaration of Indian independence and allow the Congress party to take over the internal administration of the country. This the British refused to do. As soon as the formal declaration of war was made, the Viceroy, Lord Linlithgow, without consulting any of India's leaders, pledged India's full support to Britain.

The viceroy's declaration was based on the presumption that most of India's fighting manpower came from the provinces and the people who did not support the Congress: Sikhs, Muslims, Rajputs, Gurkhas, Jats and others. The princes supported the viceroy's action by putting their armies and financial resources at the disposal of the Government.

Nehru was on the horns of a dilemma. He would have liked to lead India in the fight against fascism. He hoped and expected Britain to give him a chance to do so. But he, like the majority in the Congress party, felt that if he did not force Britain's hands to concede India its independence while it was embroiled in a war, the opportunity might not come again for a long time.

It was this sense of now-or-never on the part of the Congress and we-have-all-we-want-in-men-and-money-from-India on the part of the Government, coupled with the suspicion of Congressmen that resulted in the head-on clash between the Congress and the Government.

The British Government's attempts to negotiate with Indian leaders proved abortive. As thje war dragged on with the fascist powers victorious on all fronts, Gandhi felt the moment of truth had come. He ordered the British to "Quit India". They refused to oblige. On the morning of 9 August 1942, they simply locked up all the nationalist leaders. There was widespread rioting in many parts of India. Rail tracks were torn up; telegraph wires cut. But the administration soon got the better of the rioters.

Nehru began his last and longest incarceration. He employed his three years in gaol profitably by writing *The Discovery of India*. During these years, the tide of war turned against the fascists and his chief rival, Subhas Chandra Bose, removed himself from the Indian scene. He disappeared from his Calcutta home; some weeks later his voice was heard over Radio Berlin. And some months later he arrived in Japan to take over command of the Japanese-sponsored Indian National

Army. The exploits (largely imaginary) of the Indian National Army roused wild enthusiasm in India. In the last months of the war, Bose was killed in an air crash. All that Nehru had to play down was the fervour this fascistled soldiery had inspired among the Indian masses.

Another significant change that took place during the time Nehru was in gaol was the rise of the Muslim League. The League chief, *Qaid-e-Azam* (The Great Leader) Mohammed Ali Jinnah (d 1948) had the field to himself. He convinced the Indian Muslims that the British would soon leave India and unless they had a state of their own, the Hindus would annihilate them.

The war ended. Nehru was released from gaol in June 1945. In England, the socialists came to power. Prime Minister Attlee proclaimed that after fresh elections in India, Britain would hand over the administration to the Indians.

Nehru realised the mood of his people. He had never liked Subhas Chandra Bose and had been strongly critical of the Indian National Army. But he realised its popularity with the masses. Now that he was assured that Bose was dead, he eulogised the INA, and took up Bose's war cry "*Jai Hind*" (Victory to India) and "*Dilli Chalo*" (March to Delhi). He clamoured for the release of the thousands of INA personnel held by the British and organised the defence of three officers – a Muslim, a Hindu and a Sikh – being tried by court martial in the historic Red Fort of Delhi. The three men were convicted of treason but freed immediately. Nehru took the credit for the release of the three officers. He followed it up by an extensive tour of the country, addressed millions of people and led them in chanting slogans of the INA. The Congress swept the Hindu vote at the elections. Having achieved his objective Nehru dropped the INA like the proverbial hot potato. He supported the top brass of the army in its refusal to take back the INA personnel in the defence services.

Nehru continued to underestimate Muslim's fear of Hindu domination and their demand for a separate state of their own. The 1945 elections proved to everyone save Nehru, Gandhi, and the hard core of the Congress, that Muslims meant business. The Muslim League's only failure was in the North-West Frontier Province. But even there it had made headway.

The elation over the electoral triumph and the refusal to face Muslim separatism squarely made Nehru ride roughshod over proposals (like the one made by the British Cabinet Mission) to accommodate the Muslim point of view. India had to pay a heavy price for it.

On the eve of the transfer of power from British to Indian hands, the only one to challenge Nehru's claim to supreme leadership was Vallabhbhai Patel. It was apparent to everyone that the British would invite the President of the Congress to take over as Prime Minister of the interim government. Sardar Patel was a candidate for the presidency of the Congress. He had the backing of the conservatives and was generally regarded as a more experienced administrator than Nehru. If the members of the Congress had been left to themselves, they would have preferred to have Patel as their President or Prime Minister. At the decisive moment, Gandhi stepped in to tilt the balance in favour of Nehru. Gandhi had good reason to have reservations about Patel. Patel was an old man of seventy-two and in indifferent health. Nehru was fifty-seven and in excellent shape. Patel was somewhat narrow in his outlook *vis-à-vis* the Muslims and even distrusted the Muslim members of the Congress. "There is only one genuinely nationalist Muslim in India – Jawaharlal," he was known to have said. In the Hindu-Muslim riots that had broken out in many parts of India, Patel had expressed sympathy for the Hindus and exonerated their part in the killings as retaliation. All said and done, the urbane, sophisticated and handsome Nehru would create a better image for India than the scowling, acid-tongued, chauvinist Patel. "Jawaharlal cannot be replaced today," said Gandhi. "He, a Harrow boy, a Cambridge graduate and a barrister, is wanted to carry on the negotiations with Englishmen."

And so it was. Nehru was re-elected President of the Indian National Congress and invited by the viceroy to be the first vice-president of his executive council. Nehru's stewardship of the country during the year and a half he was head of what is generally known as the interim government was marked by further alienation of Muslims from the Hindus. The Muslim League felt that unless it demonstrated its opposition to "Congress-Hindu" rule, Muslim acquiescence might be taken for granted. A "Direct Action" day was organised on 16 August 1946.

Rioting broke out in the League-administered province of Bengal. The killings started in Calcutta and then spread to the Muslim majority district, Noakhali. Hindus took a bloody beating at the hands of Muslim hoodlums. In Bihar, where they were predominant, they wreaked terrible vengeance on the Muslims. The only man who tried to douse the fires of hate was Mahatma Gandhi. But even he could not prevent riots from assuming the proportions of a civil war.

17

Nehru as Prime Minister

*N*ehru had a feeling for words and a vision of the future. He knew what he said at a historic moment would be quoted in books of history. For such occasions he took pains to clothe his words with poetic resonance. One such speech was delivered on the night of 14 August 1947 in the Indian Constituent Assembly:

> Long years ago we made a tryst with destiny, and now the time comes when we shall redeem our pledge, not wholly or in full measure, but very substantially. At the stroke of the midnight hour, when the world sleeps, India will awake to life and freedom. A moment comes, which comes but rarely in history, when we step out from the old to the new, when an age ends, and when the soul

of a nation, long suppressed, finds utterance ...
The achievement we celebrate today is but a step,
an opening of opportunity, to the greater triumphs
and achievements that await us ... Peace has been
said to be indivisible. So is freedom, so is prosperity
now, and so also is disaster in this One World
that can no longer be split into isolated fragments.

Nehru as Prime Minister

A second occasion, when the usually rambling, at
times incoherent, Nehru showed his gift of choosing
the right words was on the assassination of Gandhi (30
January 1948). He broke the news to the people in a
broadcast over All India Radio:

Friends and comrades, the light has gone out of
our lives and there is darkness everywhere ... Our

beloved leader, Bapu as we called him, the Father of the Nation, is no more ... We will not see him again as we have seen him for these many years. We will not run to him for advice and seek solace from him, and that is a terrible blow, not to me only, but to millions and millions in this country ...

The light has gone out, I said, and yet I was wrong. For the light that shone in this country was no ordinary light. The light that has illumined this country for these many many years will illumine this country for many more years, and a thousand years later, that light will still be seen in this country and the world will see it and it will give solace to innumerable hearts. For that light represented something more than the immediate present, it represented the living, the eternal truths, reminding us of the right path, drawing us from error, taking this ancient country to freedom.

The next day, when he had more time to polish his phrases, he paid an even more eloquent tribute to Bapu in a speech to the Constituent Assembly:

How shall we praise him and how shall we measure him, because he was not of the common clay all of us are made of? ... We mourn him; we shall always mourn him, because we are human and cannot forget our beloved Master. But ... he would chide us if we merely mourn ... Let us be worthy of him.

India started its life as an independent nation with acute tension with Pakistan over, amongst other things, rioting between Hindus and Sikhs on the one side and Muslims on the other, resulting in a two-way traffic of millions of refugees across the borders. On the issue of the attitude towards Muslims, Prime Minister Nehru and Sardar Patel, who was Deputy Prime Minister holding charge of the vital portfolio of Home Affairs, were at variance. Patel distrusted the Muslims. "There are four-and-a-half crores (45 million) of Muslims in India, many of whom helped the creation of Pakistan. How can anyone believe that they have changed overnight?" he asked. Also, "Muslims say they are loyal citizens and therefore why should anybody doubt their bona fides? To them I would say, 'Why do you ask us? Search your own conscience." In the bloody business of settling scores with the Muslims, he was for taking "ten eyes for one".

At the time, Sardar Patel's suspicions of the Muslims' loyalties were shared by most Hindus and Sikhs. Besides this, Sardar Patel had earned a great name for himself for the way he had brought the Indian princes to heel and made them sign instruments of accession to the Indian Union. He was considered the abler administrator. Only two considerations prevented the "indomitable Sardar", as his admirers called him, from toppling Nehru. One was Mahatma Gandhi's unconcealed preference for Nehru; the other, Patel's own sense of patriotism. The Mahatma's assassination dissipated the prevailing fog of bitterness against the Muslims and further strengthened Nehru's hands. Two years later (15 December 1950) Patel died, leaving Nehru undisputed leader of the country.

★

Nehru was Prime Minister of India for eighteen years till his death on 27 May 1964. Instead of narrating the events of his tenure in the chronological order, it would be more profitable to examine his contribution to shaping his country.

Nehru played the dominant role in making India a secular democracy. At a time when most educated people questioned the wisdom of imposing a democratic constitution on a people reared on monarchical traditions, where there were such vast disparities of wealth between the few who were the richest men of the world and the millions who were the world's poorest, and where barely one out of ten could read or sign his name, Nehru's reasoning partook of the nature of a religious conviction in the good sense of the people. One did not have to be educated or prosperous to know whom to vote for any more than one had to be a cobbler to know where the shoe pinched.

The details of drawing up the Constitution were left to the leader of the untouchables, Dr B.R. Ambedkar, who was Law Minister, and the driving force was Nehru. The Constitution was based on the Government of India Act of 1935. Embellished with a high-sounding preamble, "We the peoples of India ..." it stated the objectives towards which India would strive and guaranteed freedom of speech, association, religion, property, etc., etc., as fundamental rights of the people. The pattern was British; with an elected Prime Minister charged with the governance of the country; the President was to be a figurehead to discharge ceremonial functions. It was a federal Constitution empowering the states of the Union to have their own elected legislatures, chief ministers presiding over state cabinets of ministers charged with administering functions other than those reserved for the Centre, like defence and communications.

Nehru's faith in the good sense of the people was demonstrated in the elections. The first took place in the winter of 1951-52 when more than 105 million men and women (60 per cent of the electorate) cast their votes. Since then Indians have gone to the polls in increasing numbers showing a maturity of political judgement that belied the gloomy prophecy "it-won't-work-in-India" made by India-denigrators. India is the world's largest democracy. Outside the British Commonwealth, the Scandinavian countries, Japan and the United States, no people enjoy greater freedom to speak their minds.

Nehru was chiefly instrumental in persuading his countrymen to continue their association with the British Commonwealth. The manner in which the English relinquished power by ramming it down the throats of unbelieving Indians cured Indians of their Anglophobia and changed it into a nostalgic pro-British sentimentalism. Nehru was a pragmatist: he realised that by retaining membership of the "Old boys club", India would have many advantages; by opting out of it, it would gain nothing. Hence though on 26 January 1950 India declared itself a sovereign, democratic republic, it retained its membership of the Commonwealth.

An equally large radical stride forward, for which credit must be given to Nehru, was the introduction of the Hindu Code, granting rights of property to Hindu women, outlawing polygamy and legalising divorce. At the time, there was hardly any women's movement clamouring for these rights and a considerable body of male opposition to such a move. Nehru steamrollered the traditionalists by staking his Government's future on the issue and had the bill passed into law. The result has been incongruous: while the vast majority of Indian women continue to be illiterate, given away in marriage without being consulted, ill-treated by husbands and mothers-in-law, shunned as outcastes when widowed, a very small educated minority has availed itself of the windfall in their fortunes by getting into the legislatures, becoming chief ministers of states, cabinet ministers, governors, ambassadors and senior civil servants. In no other country in the world do so few women wield so much power as they do in the India of today.

Nehru the socialist was a strong advocate of state-planned development. The partition had dislocated the economic and industrial life of the country, the most glaring example being that of the major foreign exchange earner, jute. The jute-growing areas went to East Pakistan, the jute mills came to India. The Pakistani jute crop was wasted; Indian jute mills were idle. At the same time the seemingly ceaseless flow of refugees from Pakistan created problems of resettlement and employment. Nehru had little faith in the Indian businessman to solve these problems. He had seen the enormous profits that industrialists and contractors had made during World War II without contributing anything towards the welfare of heir workers. It was indeed a "shameful traffic in human beings and profit at the expense of the nation". Under Nehru's guidance the Government of India announced its Industrial Policy (April 1948). There was nothing alarmingly radical about it. Certain industries like armaments, atomic energy, and railways were reserved for the "public" (state-owned) sector. It was also provided that further expansion in coal, iron, steel, shipbuilding, posts and telegraphs, would be handled by the state. The rest was left to private enterprise.

In 1950 Nehru set up a Planning Commission. It started by making out a depressing catalogue of the country's abysmal poverty and backwardness: income per head 72 paise per day; expectation of life 27 years; literacy 17 per cent; 2 million unemployed, 15 million underemployed; only 1 out of every 100 villages with electric power. The First Five-Year Plan, launched in 1951, laid stress on agricultural regeneration: dams, powerhouses, canals, and under a Community Project Scheme launched in October 1952, the opening up of villages by link roads. The plan was successfully completed before its time. A Second Five-Year Plan (1956-61) to achieve the same measure of success in industry did not go as well as the first. It relied heavily on foreign aid and the import of foreign machinery. The increasing tension in the Middle East, and the need to arm against the growing menace of China, threw a spanner in the works. By then the Congress party had also taken a more dogmatic line on socialism. At its session in Avadi in 1955, a precise limit was placed on the role of the private sector: it was to have no more than a third of the share of industry. Thereafter, the Five-Year Plans went off the rails.

One aspect of planning which Nehru ignored was the need to limit the size of the population. He continued to believe that talk of "population explosion" was capitalist propaganda. Even when the multiplication tables clearly proved that whatever advances India made in raising more food and in providing other amenities would be cancelled out by the increase in the number of consumers, Nehru persisted in giving birth control a low priority. As late as 1958 he told his biographer, Michael Brecher, "The question of limiting the family is not the primary question. We have to make economic progress much more rapidly and we cannot wait for family planning to bring results. Also the rate of population growth in India is not high: India can support a large population given economic growth." Thus India, with barely 2.4 per cent of the world's land surface, was expected to support 14 per cent of the world's population, increasing at a rate of 2.5 per cent every year.

Nehru did not pretend to be a pacifist as Gandhi did. But many steps taken during Nehru's regime destroyed the image of India as the land of Gandhi. First, there was the conflict with Pakistan over Kashmir. India's position was initially both morally and legally sound. When the Maharajah of Kashmir desired accession of India, Nehru chose to consult the leader of the Kashmir people, Sheikh Abdullah, who was then in prison, and only after getting his consent, accepted accession of the state. Pakistan, on the other hand, tried to force the issue by conniving an invasion of the state by armed tribesmen and then moving its army in support. India had every right to defend Kashmir. In the war that followed, more than half the state was taken over by Pakistan. The dividing line continues to be what it was when a cease-fire was agreed to on 1 January 1948. But Nehru gave a solemn undertaking that when conditions returned to normal, the wishes of the people of Kashmir would be ascertained. Conditions have never returned to normal, but there is little doubt in anyone's mind that the vast majority of the people of Kashmir do not wish to continue to be a part of India except as an autonomous, near-independent state. India has stalled a decision on Kashmir and as a result been unable to normalize its relations with Pakistan.

The manner in which the state of Hyderabad was taken over (1948) and the Portuguese enclaves of Goa, Daman and Diu annexed (December 1961), eroded the image of India as Gandhi-land. A series of border incidents were created in Hyderabad to justify the Indian army marching in to restore order, which was euphemistically described as a "police action". The same procedure of generating tension and spreading wildly exaggerated stories of a build-up of Portuguese naval and armed strength was used to justify the take-over of Goa, Daman and Diu. Neither in Hyderabad nor in the Portuguese possessions did the resistance offered lend credence to Indian propaganda.

Another of Nehru's miscalculations for which the country had to pay a heavy price was underestimating the mischief that could be caused by squabbles over languages. As early as 1920 the Indian National Congress had passed a resolution that as soon as the British left, the boundaries of the states would be re-drawn on the basis of languages spoken in the regions. Nehru had no doubt in his mind that linguistic disputes were an artificial creation of the British. Soon after 1948 he appointed a commission to examine the subject. Both the Dar Commission and another set up by the Congress expressed themselves against tampering with state boundaries. How grossly Nehru and his advisers misjudged the sentiment of the people for their languages was proved by savage riots that broke out in 1953 over the demand for a separate state by Telugu-speaking people. Andhra was conceded under pressure of this agitation. And yet another body, the States Reorganisation Commission, was constituted to re-examine the subject. The Commission submitted its report in 1955. In 1956 riots broke out in Bombay demanding a separate state for the Marathi-speaking people. The riots spread to Gujarat. The old state was divided into Maharashtra and Gujarat (May 1961). Then agitation flared up in the Punjab where the Sikhs demanded a "Punjabi *Suba*" (where, incidentally, Sikhs would form a majority of the population). Nehru strenuously opposed the Punjabi *Suba*. But once having conceded the principle, the administration had always to be on the defensive. The Punjabi *Suba* had to be conceded in 1965, resulting in a further readjustment of boundaries between Himachal Pradesh, Haryana and Punjab.

The linguistic cancer has not been contained. Agitations for recognition of dialects as languages and separate administrative units for them continue. Much worse, the insistence by the states that administration be conducted in regional languages has created problems of communications with the centre and other states. A fostered regional chauvinism now threatens the integrity of the country.

Nehru's greatest contribution was to outline the principles of India's foreign policy. As a socialist he was allergic to the colonial powers and friendly to communist countries like Soviet Russia and China who were also India's neighbours. At the same time he realised the necessity of getting aid from the US and the Commonwealth. He embarked on a policy of non-alignment designed to stay friendly with the two opposing power blocs and build and third neutral bloc consisting of the newly-independent nations of Asia and Africa. He wrote: "A policy must be in keeping with the traditional background and temper of the country. It should be idealistic. If it becomes one of sheer opportunism it is not realistic, then it is likely to be adventurist and wholly ineffective." In an interview with Michael Brecher, he said: "Ideological urges obviously play some part … especially in a democracy because … no policy can go very far if it is quite divorced from the people's thinking. However, in the final analysis, all foreign policy concerns itself chiefly with the national interest of the country concerned." As for India's foreign policy, he said: "Apart from our desire for peace, it is our feeling that peace is absolutely essential for our progress and our growth. And with the coming of nuclear weapons, war seems to us – and seems to most people everywhere – extreme folly, that is, it has ceased to promise what you want."

Furthermore, "I would say that non-alignment is a policy which is nationally profitable for any country. But in some cases there is danger – because of the smallness of the country or because of its geographical position – that, whether it is aligned or non-aligned, it may suffer from the war."

For a while this policy, enshrined in the five principles called *Panchsheela*, yielded handsome dividends. India as the great developing, uncommitted power, played the role of peacemaker in Korea, Indo-China and the Middle East. Then Nehru's innate dislike for America's "economic imperialism" made him veer towards the socialist bloc. The final disillusionment, however, came not from imperialists but from socialists. India, which never ceased from criticising the US involvement in Vietnam, did not have a word to say against Soviet Russia's violent intervention in Hungary (1956). When communist China occupied Tibet (1961) all Nehru did was to make some noises of protest and accord an ungracious welcome to the Dalai Lama and the refugees who followed him into India. His attempt to contain Chinese expansionism in the autumn of 1962 resulted in a disaster to Indian arms. The Chinese streamed over the seemingly impassable Himalayan ranges, driving the ill-equipped Indian troops into the plains. It was not Soviet Russia but the United States and the Commonwealth countries that came to India's help. Nehru candidly admitted the failure of his foreign policy: "We have been living in a fool's paradise," he said.

After the defeat at the hands of the Chinese, Nehru was never the same man. His health deteriorated, his mind began to wander; he would fall asleep at official banquets. There was open criticism of his reliance on men like Krishna Menon and Sardar Panikkar, who had little to commend themselves except their loquacity; his misplaced sense of loyalty to old friends (Krishna Menon, T.T. Krishnamachari) which made him retain them in office even after they had been clearly shown to have misled him; his continued patronage of colleagues who had been proved to have resorted to corrupt practices – Pratap Singh Kairon, T.T. Krishnamachari, Bakshi Ghulam Mohammed, Biju Patnaik, and many others. His charisma, the affection the people had for him, and the absence of anyone who could replace him compelled Nehru to stay as Prime Minister for another two years till he died on 27 May 1964.

18

Indira Gandhi

*P*eople asked three questions about Indira Gandhi. What kind of woman was she? How did she become the most powerful woman in the history of the world? Where did she lead India?

Amateur psychiatrists will probe Indira's childhood days to find clues to her character. Indira was the only child of a frail mother and a dominant, dynamic father. Close relatives – notably grandfather Motilal, and aunt Vijayalakshmi – and many visitors to the house were people of national stature. All this must have created feelings of anxiety and misgivings that she might not measure up to these people. The frequent visitations by the police to take away her parents must have added to the feeling of insecurity and turned the

marbled grandeur of Anand
Bhavan into a palace haunted
by unfriendly spirits. All she had
for company was distant
relatives, servants and her dolls.
Hence the combination of
paradoxes – daydreams of
greatness ("When I was very
small I looked up to Joan of Arc
as my hero.") offset by

Indira Gandhi

nightmares of doubt regarding her ability to attain that
greatness; a craving for affection offset by distrust of
affection because the people she loved and wanted to
be loved by often withdrew from her world and left
her in agonising loneliness.

These must have been some of the emotions that
moulded this child born on 19 November 1917, under
the sign of Scorpio. A Scorpio child, say astrologers,
is quarrelsome, callous, hardworking and clever at
making money. Indira had none of these traits. Sarojini
Naidu was closer to the truth in her telegram of
congratulations to the Nehrus when she described
Indira as "the soul of new India". And she was aptly
named Priyadarshini – lovely to behold.

Indira's education was as haphazard as her
childhood. She was in and out of schools and changed
tutors as she had to move from one town to another.
Her father's letters from gaol were no doubt a kind of
correspondence course in history. But most of the

reading was done by her with spasmodic guidance· from different people. She never stayed in any educational institution long enough to gain anything substantial from it: no lasting friendships, no pupil-teacher attachments, not even a diploma. She went in and out of Shanti Niketan, the International School at Geneva, Badminton, and a few months at Somerville College in Oxford. If she had applied for a job in the Government of India – of which she was the top executive – she would not qualify even for the post of a clerk in the lowest grade. All she had to her credit on paper was having passed the matriculation examination (division unknown) of the University of Bombay.

It is not surprising that many people who met Indira in her teens were not impressed by her. Mrs Laski described her as a "mousy, shy little girl who didn't seem to have any political ideas". Reginald Sorensen confessed that she made no impression on him "except as the reflection of her father".

It was about this time that she spoke to her biographer, Khwaja Ahmed Abbas, of her ambitions in life. "I would have liked to be a writer. I would have liked to do research in history, or perhaps in anthropology, for that interests me even more than history… If I wanted to have an easy life, I could have become an interior decorator – I am really interested in the subject … I could have even become a dancer (she certainly had the looks and the figure) – I learnt

Manipuri in Shanti Niketan." But she wasted little time on writing, anthropology, interior decoration or dancing. Politics was in her blood. She found fulfilment in the rough and tumble of political life.

Indira came into practical politics without any clear notions of political theory. She was reared in a fuzzy atmosphere of Fabian socialism, which was more a passionate championship of the underdog than a precisely thought-out political creed to which a label could be attached. "I don't have a political philosophy," she admitted to an interviewer, Welles Hangen, author of *After Nehru, Who?* He sneered, "She, like her father, is a case of arrested ideological development, clinging to outworn Fabian dialectics, tilting at vested interests, and forever invoking the Utopia of socialistic nationalism. She has the reputation of being more radical and incisive than her father, but this is hardly surprising. Youth can afford to be incisive and radicalism always flourishes best without responsibility."

Indira's socialism had many origins. The seed was sown by her father, it was nurtured by associates of her formative years: workers of the India League whom she befriended; Krishna Menon, Feroze Gandhi (whom she later married), Minoo Masani, Mohan Kumaramangalam, Rajni Patel, Bhupesh Gupta, Jyoti Basu. Revulsion against fascism, which was at the time ascendant in Europe, and admiration of what she saw of Soviet Russia confirmed her in her faith. While some of her college-day associates accepted Marxism, she like many of her equally affluent friends did not find it necessary to spell out socialism. It was at best a pill to banish bad dreams of suffering humanity and ensure sound sleep in air-conditioned comfort. How nice to be able to label yourself as pro-poor and progressive and decry others as rich and reactionary!

On her return home Indira was sucked into the vortex of Indian politics. Marriage to Feroze Gandhi (1942) may have for some time diverted her attention. But not for long. For one, an essential element of her affection for Feroze was his unbounded admiration of her parents and identity of political views. What's more, since he, like her father and other relatives, was bent on courting imprisonment, she could hardly be expected to settle down as a *hausfrau*. She was born into a political household and married a political husband. The "Quit India" movement claimed her entire family including herself. She received her first baptism in blood: she was beaten by the police. In gaol, she was treated like an ordinary C class convict. Although ill (she had kidney trouble and an attack of pleurisy in her young days), the discourtesy shown to her by her jailers (they ate up mangoes sent for her) did not embitter her. She stood the ordeal manfully.

The end of the war brought a complete change in the pattern of Indira's life. Her father became Prime Minister. She persuaded her husband to move to Delhi to be near her widowed father. Her husband soon became a figure of considerable political importance and was elected to Parliament. They drifted apart. He moved out to an apartment of his own; she moved into the Prime Minister's House to become his confidante-secretary-nurse-housekeeper. Most of her time was occupied in fulfilling these roles; the rest in looking after her two growing sons.

Inevitably, Indira Gandhi became the chief means of communication with the Prime Minister and was cultivated by cabinet ministers, chief ministers, ambitious politicians and civil servants. She was made a member of many committees, began to receive and entertain visiting dignitaries, accompanied her father to the Commonwealth Prime Ministers' Conferences in London, on state visits to the US, the USSR, China, and to the Panchsheel Conference in Bandung.

During the four years 1955-59, Nehru discreetly put the Congress party machine in the hands of his daughter. She was elected a member of the Congress Working Committee; then of the Congress Parliamentary Board meant to select candidates for the two houses of Parliament, and finally of the Congress Election Committee to perform the same function for the states' legislatures. It was not surprising that in 1959 she was elected President of the All-India Congress Committee – to become the third Nehru and the fourth woman in the history of the organisation to be its head. it was during her tenure as President that her public image as a shadow of her father and husband changed to one of a leader with a mind and determination of her own. Leftist? Maybe, but with no firm commitments. She was instrumental in the dismissal of the communist ministry (July 1959) which had been in power in Kerala for almost two years. She had no compunction in making alliances with other parties, including the much-hated Muslim League. In May 1961, she sanctioned the breakup of Bombay State into Maharashtra and Gujarat.

Events helped her rise to pre-eminence. In 1960, Feroze Gandhi died. Two years later there was widespread Hindu-Muslims rioting in central India. Indira toured these areas reassuring Muslims of her support. The Muslims, India's most important minority, were convinced that after Nehru, his daughter was their best hope. In the autumn of 1962 came the war with China. One of the top leaders who bothered to visit the border areas was Indira Gandhi, the other being Lal Bahadur Shastri. The army also realised she was their best bet. The defeat reduced Nehru's public image and removed men like Krishna Menon (then Defence Minister) and General B.M. Kaul (Field Commander) from the list of contenders for Nehru's throne. Another serious rival, Morarji Desai, had been eliminated in 1963 in a purge known as the Kamaraj Plan to refurbish the image of the Congress party.

In May 1964, when Nehru died, Indira Gandhi was high on the list of likely successors. She bided her time. Lal Bahadur Shastri became Prime Minister, defeating his chief rival, Morarji Desai. Indira was made Minister of Information and Broadcasting, ranking fourth in the Cabinet.

Indira Gandhi's tenure as Minister of Information and Broadcasting was not very distinguished. Although AIR news and commentaries were liberalised and the Films Division was given a boost, most of this was due to the fact that she was often away from Delhi and the departments were left to competent civil servants. She shelved the most important issue of making AIR into a public corporation by simply appointing a commission. (As Prime Minister, she ignored the commission's recommendations.) Although she continued to be held in esteem as the daughter of the great Jawaharlal, her reputation as an administrator suffered. But before much damage could be done, fate came to her rescue. The Indo-Pak war of September 1965 had magnified the image of the diminutive Lal Bahadur Shastri to one of formidable proportions. But no sooner did that happen than Shastri died at Tashkent on 11 January 1966. The hunt for his successor began.

It took a few days after Shastri's death for people to realise that there was no choice, save Indira Gandhi. The cabal of kingmakers were all too eager to become kings themselves and in the process cancelled out each other's chances. Indira Gandhi alone retained her public image as one who did not seek power but was reluctantly agreeable to having it thrust upon her. All her rivals suffered from some crippling defect: faddism (Morarji); obscurantism (Nanda); regional patriotism (Chavan); lack of sophistication (Kamaraj). She alone was free of these taints and was, in addition, the only one of the contenders who could meet leaders of other nations on their level. A foreign correspondent put it succinctly: "She is India's best bet, look at the others and you know it has to be her."

And so it was. What self-styled kingmakers proposed, the chief ministers of the states disposed. Indira Gandhi trounced Morarji Desai by 355 to 189 votes, and became, on 19 January 1966 the first woman Prime Minister of India – the second woman in 700 years, after Razia Sultana, to become a ruler of Hindustan.

★

Of Indira Gandhi it could be said that she was not only born into greatness, she also achieved greatness and while enjoying it had more greatness thrust upon her.

The legacy that Nehru and Shastri left to Indira Gandhi was a bed of thorns. The five-year plans had gone awry; both agricultural and industrial production was at a low ebb and India's foreign exchange reserves at rock bottom. Corruption was rampant. Nevertheless Indira Gandhi gave first priority to international acceptance of her as the new leader of India. She undertook an extensive tour of Europe and the United States.

She got back into the saddle and within a few months left no doubt in anyone's mind that she was the boss. Without consulting her senior colleagues (neither Queen-maker Kamaraj nor the chief pretender Morarji Desai), she announced the devaluation of the rupee by 57 per cent in June 1966. She conceded the Sikh claim for a Punjabi Suba in which they would form a majority of the population, ignoring the fact that her father and most other Indian leaders had strenuously opposed this demand. And when right-wing Hindu parties clashed with the Government over the question of banning the slaughter of cows, she utilised the rioting that followed as an excuse to sack her Home Minister, Gulzarilal Nanda – a man who had twice acted as Prime Minister and had been promised by his soothsayers that he was India's man of destiny.

None of these moves brought credit to the ruling party. The results of the General Elections of 1967 showed what the people thought of the Congress. The Congress lost over a hundred seats in Parliament: stalwarts like Kamaraj, Atulya Ghosh and S.K. Patil were unseated. The party was left with a slender majority of forty. The swing to the right (Swatantra and Bharatiya Jan Sangh) was marked at the Centre as it was in the states, many of which came to be ruled by opposition parties.

Mrs Gandhi realised that she had to get rid of the "Old Guard" conservatives before she could hope to regain the popularity that her party had once enjoyed.

The first trial of strength came over the choice of successor to retiring President Radhakrishnan. Mrs Gandhi's choice was the Muslim Vice-President, Zakir Husain. The opposition parties, assured of support from some of Mrs Gandhi's followers, put up the then Chief Justice of the Supreme Court, Justice Subba Rao. Zakir Husain won and became the first Muslim President of the Republic.

The internal situation continued to deteriorate; in Bengal an extreme left-wing faction of the communists, known as the Naxalites (from the town of Naxalbari where they first tried to set up a communist government) spread terror in the state. In Calcutta alone the average toll of life taken by these political thugs was from five to a dozen every day. Nevertheless, in the state elections, the Bengal United Front consisting of a combination of leftist parties captured 210 of the 280 seats, leaving the Congress a meagre 55. The Congress also took a drubbing in the Punjab where the right-wing Akalis won a decisive majority to form a government.

Indira Gandhi had good reasons to ascribe the reverses to the Congress being a house divided against itself. At its session in Faridabad near Delhi, the party President, Nijalingappa, had openly criticised public sector enterprises. Mrs Gandhi had countered it by giving a pep-talk on "social purpose" to the industrialists and members of the Federation of Indian Chambers of Commerce and Industry. But by now the opposition to Mrs Gandhi within the party had been strengthened by the return of Kamaraj and S.K. Patil to Parliament. They – known at the time as "the Syndicate" – began to muster forces behind Morarji Desai. Not to be outdone, Mrs Gandhi's supporters, notably Chandrashekhar, exposed shady financial deals carved out by Morarji Desai's son, Kanti Desai, while his father was Union Finance Minister.

The year 1969 was the year of the Great Divide in the ranks of the Congress. In May, President Zakir Husain suddenly died. The collision came over the choice of the successor. At its session in Bangalore, "the Syndicate"-dominated Board voted for N. Sanjiva Reddy. Mrs Gandhi demurred. When Nijalingappa wanted to issue a whip in support of Sanjiva Reddy, she came out for a "free vote" and openly expressed her support for the candidature of vice-president V.V. Giri. "I feel that the issues involved go beyond the presidential poll," she said. She had the foresight to elevate the contest from a personal issue between the Syndicate's Sanjiva Reddy and Mrs Gandhi's V.V. Giri to one of economic and political policies. At the Bangalore session she gave expression to what she described as "stray thoughts jotted down in a hurry" which included such items as limitation of "unproductive expenditure and conspicuous consumption of corporate bodies", nationalisation of financial institutions, shutting out big business from the monopoly of producing consumer goods, changes in agrarian laws to limit holdings of land, etc. And in July she announced the nationalisation of fourteen banks.

The Congress party split into two – the "Cong (O)" consisting of the Old Guard with at least two states, Gujarat and Mysore, on one side, and the "Cong (I)" (Indira's Congress) with a slender edge over its rivals in Parliament and the remaining Congress states. Giri won by a very narrow margin: the leftist parties and the DMK of Tamil Nadu, the Akalis of the Punjab and the Bharatiya Kranti Dal supported him. In a frenzy of mutual recrimination, Nijalingappa expelled Indira Gandhi and her henchmen from the party. They formed a party of their own with Subramaniam as their president. Mrs Gandhi forced Morarji Desai out of her cabinet. Four senior ministers including Dr Ram Subhag Singh, later the leader of the party in opposition, resigned in protest. The purge and defections reduced her following in Parliament to a minority. She had to rely on the support of the communists as well as the DMK, the Akalis and the BKD to keep her government going.

The battle was once again joined in 1970. Mrs Gandhi's Congress chose Jagjivan Ram as President for the AICC session in Bombay. The Cong (O) made much of the information leaked earlier that Jagjivan Ram had not paid his income tax for ten years. But the Cong (I) ignored these personal attacks and launched a plan of making the country socialist by abolishing the privy purses of the princes (by amending the Constitution and, when that was overruled by the Supreme Court, by Presidential ordinance), by curbing monopolies of big industrial houses and imposing a ceiling of thirty acres on holdings of land.

Indira Gandhi displayed all her cunning and stamina in the general elections she called a year before they were due. She made alliances with the communists, the DMK, the Muslim League and the Bangla Congress. She toured the entire country addressing as many as fourteen meetings a day. She spoke to 20 million people, rarely sleeping more than three to four hours in the night. All that the opposition had to offer the electorate was the negative "*Indira hatao*" (get rid of Indira); by contrast Indira at least offered a slogan of hope "*garibi hatao*" (get rid of poverty).

The election was a veritable Indira wave. She won 350 seats in Parliament – 120 more than before. The CPM was able to get 24; all the other opposition parties were decimated. What helped her to win was the spectre of instability at the Centre and the overwhelming support she received from the post-1947 generation who cast their vote for the first time.

Mrs Gandhi used her great majority to remould her party and the country to her heart's desire. She sacked seven Cabinet ministers, took over the Home and the Information and Broadcasting portfolios for herself. She sacked four chief ministers of states whose support to her had not been as unqualified as she had desired.

She pushed through a series of amendments to the Constitution, including one giving Parliament the right to alter fundamental rights. She created new states: Himachal Pradesh, Meghalaya, Tripura and Arunachal Pradesh.

In March 1971 came the crisis in East Pakistan, with serious repercussions on India. As the West Pakistani military dictatorship under President Yahya Khan cracked down on Mujibur Rehman's Awami League, large numbers of refugees trekked into neighbouring Indian states. By the autumn of 1971 there were as many as 12 million Pakistanis in Indian refugee camps. Mrs Gandhi appealed to the nations of the world to stop the genocide in East Pakistan and to help her government feed, clothe and house the millions that had sought shelter in India. She visited the USSR, Europe and the United States to plead her case. The response was very poor. In December 1971, the Indian army moved into East Pakistan to go to the help of the Mukti Bahini freedom-fighters of Bangladesh and thus forced Pakistan to declare war against India (3 December 1971). The Indian army won a decisive victory on both fronts, destroying Pakistan's military machine in barely two weeks of fighting. The credit for the victory rightly went to Indira Gandhi. She was given the highest honour the country could offer – Bharat Ratna – the jewel of India.

Indira Gandhi cashed in on her immense popularity to wipe out the remnants of the Opposition. In the state elections of 1972 her party again swept the polls by winning 1926 seats of the 2529 that it contested. She became the supreme ruler of the country, with the backhanded compliment – Queen Empress of India.

No woman in the history of the world held the destinies of so many millions of people in her hands as did Mrs Indira Gandhi. The awesome concentration of power was fraught with serious consequences to the functioning of democracy in India. Some of these had already begun to manifest themselves. With the total – and it would appear wilful – elimination of other popularly chosen leaders, Mrs Gandhi had begun to turn for counsel to men and women of her own choice and civil servants who were not answerable to Parliament. Ever since she became Prime Minister she had sought advice from what is pejoratively described as her kitchen cabinet. The personnel of this inner coterie had often changed from junior ministers in the earlier years to the predominance of civil servants in the later. As a consequence, from a constitutional system designed on the British pattern, where a Prime Minister leads his team of elected Cabinet ministers, Mrs Gandhi was veering towards the Presidential system of the United States in which the Chief Executive picks his counsellors from wherever he likes. The United States Constitution and convention provide many checks on the President's powers. These do not exist in the Indian Constitution. As a result, instead of getting honest responsible advice from leaders who carried weight in Parliament and with the people, Mrs Gandhi had surrounded herself with a bunch of clever sycophants eager to express agreement with her views.

The office of the President suffered a diminution of status. It was India's misfortune that at a time when she had the most powerful of the three Prime Ministers in its quarter century of independence, she should have the weakest of its four Presidents. Rajendra Prasad (1950-62), Radhakrishnan (1962-67) and Zakir Husain (1967-69) were all men of considerable stature, whose opinions were respected by Nehru, Shastri and Indira Gandhi. Giri did not have the academic distinctions of his predecessors and was essentially a creature of the Prime Minister. He did as he was bidden to do. More often, to avoid embarrassment, he was left to perform ceremonial functions and to enjoy the comforts of the presidential palace.

A somewhat similar diminution of status had resulted in the post of governors of states. The posts went to discredited politicians or were given as rewards to faithful (not necessarily distinguished) civil servants and generals on retirement. As a result, state chief ministers, when they were at variance with their governors, ignored or isolated them in their Raj Bhavans. The Central government used the governors as its agents – informers who could, when the necessity arose, dissolve a ministry to administer the state under President's (actually the Prime Minister's) rule.

Once the President and the governors began to act as functionaries of the Prime Minister, the Central government tended to arrogate power to itself and reduce federalism to mere form. In many states of India there were powerful movements for more autonomy, e.g., in Kashmir, Punjab, Nagaland and Tamil Nadu. These movements could best be contained by a loose rather than a restrictive federalism. If thwarted by the Centre, the demand for autonomy could, and at times had, become a demand for separate statehood.

More sinister were the many amendments to the Constitution which qualified the citizens' right to property and which threatened freedom of speech. The administration successfully imposed a ceiling on holdings of agricultural land – the maximum any one individual could own being thirty acres – and many states enacted legislation limiting urban holdings to under rupees five lakh. It became abundantly evident that the concept of property was undergoing a communist orientation.

The Government established a stranglehold on media of mass communication. Radio and television became a government monopoly. News agencies were heavily indebted to the Government; newsprint was allocated by the Government; printing machinery could only be imported after a licence was obtained from the Government; the Government became the largest single advertiser in the press and many times used this financial thumbscrew to bring recalcitrant papers to heel. A government-inspired campaign had been launched against the "monopoly press" owned by industrial houses like the Goenkas' *Express* chain, the Jains' *Times of India* group, the Birlas' *Hindustan Times* and the Tatas' *Statesman*. "In no other country in the world except India does industry own the press," said Mrs Gandhi in justification of the measures to "nationalise" the national press. A bill to "diffuse ownership" of the big chains of papers was to be introduced in Parliament, soon. That would end the freedom of the Indian press.

With the Government's progressive encroachment over industry, hotels, retail trades and almost every other form of commercial activity, the bureaucracy grew to mammoth proportions. The Government became the largest employer.

In international relations the most significant change introduced by Mrs Gandhi was to end the non-alignment strenuously pursued by her predecessors and align India with the Soviet Union. In the past 35 years India has received massive aid from the United States, West Germany and countries of the Commonwealth. Even in critical periods, such as during the confrontation with China in 1962, while the USSR kept aloof, President Kennedy sent massive supplies of arms to India; Britain offered similar aid. It was in India's confrontations with Pakistan that these countries remained neutral, while the Soviet Union supported India. The Indo-Soviet Friendship Treaty, signed in the autumn of 1971, assured India of powerful backing, ensured success in liberating Bangladesh and defeating Pakistan.

Mrs Gandhi's immediate problems were internal. After many years of favourable monsoons which generated the Green Revolution, there was widespread drought in the summer of 1972, resulting in famine conditions in many parts of the country. Prices of essentials – wheat, rice, edible oils, kerosene, cloth – went spiralling beyond the pockets of the impoverished citizenry. It was a sad revelation that after all the slogan-mongering of *garibi hatao*, more than half the population of the country (56 per cent) lived below the subsistence level; over 60 million had no homes: they lived in slums, slept on pavements; nearly 2.5 million were unemployed and an equal number underemployed. It was not surprising that agitation became widespread. There were more strikes than ever before, more *gheraos* (blocking entrances and exits), more *bandhs* (stoppage of work), rioting, arson and open defiance of the law. For the first time in her six years of rule it appeared that the men and women whom Mrs Gandhi had carried on her triumphant band-wagon had neither the ability to resolve economic and social problems, nor were they able to persuade the people to eschew violent methods of protest and, worst of all, when faced with deliberate defiance of authority, they exhibited a species of gutlessness which branded them as utterly unfit to rule.

★

On 14 November 1974 Indira Gandhi celebrated her fifty-seventh birthday. The following fourteen years of her life were more crowded with events than those since she first appeared on the scene as a national leader. They also showed her strength and her weaknesses in the face of difficult situations. They saw the emergence of her younger son, Sanjay, as a formidable contender for succession, and the national upsurge against corruption and misrule led by Jayaprakash Narayan. In Parliament, charges of large-scale corruption were made against L.N. Mishra, Chief Minister of Bihar and undue favours shown by Bansi Lal, Chief Minister of Haryana to Sanjay Gandhi's Maruti car project. "If you catch the *bachchda* (calf), the cow is bound to follow," the wily Chief Minister is alleged to have said, referring to his growing influence on Sanjay's mother. Administration came to a halt. For weeks schools and colleges remained closed, strikes and lockouts crippled large sections of Industry. Smuggling and black marketing became rampant. It was an opportune moment for the Opposition to hit at Indira Gandhi's regime.

A massive students movement began in Gujarat and spread to different parts of the country. Jayaprakash Narayan now hailed as Lok Nayak – leader of the people, took over its leadership. Life in many cities was disrupted by *gheraos* and *bandhs*. To add to Mrs Gandhi's troubles, her election to the Lok Sabha was invalidated by Justice Sinha of the Allahabad High Court on a technical charge of corrupt practice committed by one of her election agents. She appealed to the Supreme Court. Justice Krishna Iyer partly accepted her plea. She could sit in the Lok Sabha but not have the right to vote.

Then Jayaprakash Narayan played into her hands. Students in Gujarat had *gheraoed* the legislative assembly to prevent legislators from entering it. Jayaprakash called for a similar *gherao* of the Central Parliament. This would have brought an essential part of a democratic process to a complete halt.

Mrs Gandhi decided to strike. On 26 June 1975 she proclaimed a state of national emergency and arrested all the top opposition leaders including Jayaprakash Narayan and Morarji Desai. Thousands of others were put behind bars; many others including George Fernandes went underground. Strict censorship was clamped on the press.

The initial response to the imposition of Emergency was favourable. Schools, colleges and other public institutions reopened. Factories began working fulltime, prices of essential goods came down, black marketers and smugglers were put in jails. Trains and planes began to run on schedule. It was evident that Indians respect the rod and democracy had not yet taken deep roots. Virtually the only organised resistence to the emergency regime was put up by the Akalis who kept a passive resistance movement going all through the two years it lasted. All top Akali leaders were gaoled.

As months rolled by, Congress politicians and the police began to misuse the extraordinary powers entrusted to them. Anyone they did not like got the midnight knock on his door to be taken to jail. There was no *habeas corpus*, no appeal against unjust detention. Sanjay Gandhi who had suffered much at the hands of the Opposition assumed the role of the Supreme Commander. Besides settling scores with his erstwhile adversaries, he got the opportunity to put his pet ideas into practice. He wanted to clear city slums and build healthy tenements amidst greenery. And he wanted to pursue family planning programmes with vigour. He was an impatient young man with little concern for democratic norms and the time-consuming procedures of law courts. Slums of Delhi were raised to the ground by bulldozers. Targets were set for family planners in every district and those with more than three children bullied into having themselves sterilised. Vastly exaggerated stories of the unmarried and the old who were forced into *nasbandi* spread like the proverbial wildfire. A strong resentment against the emergency regime began to build up.

Mrs Gandhi remained blissfully unaware of the erosion of her popularity. Her sycophantic counsellors and information agencies assured her that the vast majority of the population approved of the Emergency and, if she lifted it, she would get a thumping majority in her favour. In January 1977 Mrs Gandhi released all political prisoners and announced a general election.

The results of the election proved an absolute disaster for the Congress party. It was routed in every state. Mrs Gandhi lost her seat to a political buffoon, Raj Narayan. Everyone believed that Mrs Gandhi's political career had ended. She proved everyone wrong.

The Janata Government headed by Morarji Desai took office. His two seniormost colleagues Chaudhary Charan Singh and Babu Jagjivan Ram both aspired to be Prime Ministers. Instead of getting on with the task of governance entrusted to them by the electorate, the three jockeyed for the top post and wasted their time persecuting Mrs Gandhi and her son. Several Commissions of Enquiry were instituted to look into the "misdeeds" of the Gandhi family and their supporters. Then followed a series of arrests, climaxed by the arrest of Indira Gandhi herself on 3 October 1977. She was released unconditionally the next day because the magistrate found nothing substantial in the charges against her. Public furore created by the maladroit handling of Mrs Gandhi's arrest caused loss of face to the Janata Government and the arresting spree was brought to halt temporarily.

Public opinion began to turn in favour of Mrs Gandhi. As the cracks in the Janata Government widened, Mrs Gandhi toured the country, apologised for excesses committed by officials during the emergency and promised them a better deal. The tide began to turn in Mrs Gandhi's favour. In August 1978 she was elected to the Lok Sabha from Chikmagalur. (Her election was declared void and she was expelled from the House in January 1979.) A special Court was set up to speed up cases filed against her and her son, Sanjay.

By the spring of 1979 it became evident that Morarji Desai's days as Prime Minister, and of the rag-tag collection which formed his Cabinet, were numbered. They had proved totally inept in handling the problems of the country. The most dramatic illustration of their incompetence was the way they handled the revolt of the police and the paramilitary forces. While a national Commission headed by Dharamvira was looking into the working conditions of the 900,000 strong police force at the leisurely pace Indian Commissions are wont to, discontent that had been simmering for years came to the boil. Policemen who resisted in different parts of the country were brutally put down. The police rebellion was followed by widespread rioting between Hindus and Muslims.

The collapse of the Janata government came in the monsoon session of 1979. Raj Narain ditched Morarji Desai who was replaced by Charan Singh. He lasted a few months before, he too, was forced to quit. The Parliament was dissolved and fresh elections called. In the autumn of 1979, Mrs Gandhi and her party romped home with a comfortable majority. Sanjay Gandhi was elected to the Lok Sabha from Amethi.

It seemed as if the good old days had returned. Then tragedy struck the Gandhi family. On 23 June 1980 Sanjay was killed in an air crash. Although Mrs Gandhi recovered from the shock and had her elder son, Rajiv Gandhi, become her chief counsellor, she was no longer the iron lady of quick and firm decisions. Her relations with her daughter-in-law Maneka (Sanjay's widow) became a public scandal when she forced her and her grandson out of her house. She became petulant and suspicious of everyone around her. Two states, Assam and Punjab, declined into chaos. In Assam the students were in open revolt. In Punjab after having approved of the choice of Jarnail Singh Bhindranwale as a counterfoil to the Akalis who had been launching agitation after agitation against the Central government, she found herself confronted with Akalis and Bhindranwale on the same side. Bhindranwale's goons spread terror in the state killing innocent Hindus and Sikhs suspected of collaborating with the Government. Then Bhindranwale turned the Golden Temple into an armed camp and the *Akal Takhat* into a fortress from which he issued "hit lists" of people to be eliminated.

Mrs Gandhi lost her cool. She listened to advice of people who knew little about the Sikhs and the veneration in which they held the Golden Temple. She was grievously misinformed about the strength of Bhindranwale's men; she was told that they would lay down their arms if there was show of strength – and if they fought their resistence would be overcome within a matter of hours. She put the state under army rule and ordered it to take *Bhindranwale* dead or alive. "Operation Blue Star" was launched on 5, June 1984 when thousands of innocent pilgrims were inside the precincts of the temple paying homage to its founder, Guru Arjun Dev on the anniversary of his martyrdom. Instead of a couple of hours as anticipated, the Operation took five days. And far from surrendering in the face of show of strength, Bhindranwale and his men fought with fanatic zeal to the very last. The death toll was horrendous. The army lost several hundred jawans, the defenders and innocent pilgrims caught in the crossfire accounted for another three to five thousand dead. The *Akal Takhat* was wrecked; the temple archives reduced to ashes. The Sikhs felt deeply humiliated and became vengeful.

Mrs Gandhi was not big enough to admit that she had blundered. She had a White Paper published giving the history of her negotiations with the Akalis, the reign of terror let lose by Bhindranwale and details of "Operation Blue Star". The White Paper was dismissed by most people as a whitewash.

After Operation Blue Star, Mrs Gandhi (and those connected with the army action) were marked for destruction by Bhindranwale's supporters. Many conspiracies hatched to get her were foiled. No one had suspected that she would meet her end in her own heavily guarded home at the hands of men sworn to protect her. On the morning of 31 October 1984 two of her Sikh security guards, Beant Singh and Satwant Singh who had earlier taken vows at the Golden Temple to avenge its sacrilege, pumped pistol and sten-gun bullets into her frail body. A couple of hours later she succumbed to her injuries at the All India Institute of Medical Sciences in New Delhi.

Her gory end was followed by a pogrom of the Sikh population in towns and cities of northern India in which between five to ten thousand innocent Sikhs perished, thousands of Sikh homes looted and hundreds of crores worth of Sikh property destroyed. Thus ended the sixteen years rule of the most powerful woman monarch of all times.